T3
Train the Trainer
10 Things Every Successful Trainer Must Know

"Tavis Banks didn't just write a book, he has given us a tool that Leaders can use to build extraordinary organizations and culture. I am using this book to train my staff and improve on my Leadership. Great job Tavis. If you are serious about building yourself and organization, read this book, implement the lessons."

Dr. Will Moreland

CEO, Moreland Consulting Group

"Tavis nailed it! His knowledge, passion, and expertise as a leader in the training and development space pops off the pages of this book to make their training engaging, memorable and useful!
Each chapter of this amazing book includes a handful of excellent, well-thought-tip, tools, and resources for trainers, educators, and leaders thirsting for innovative ways to make their training memorable and useful! Well done."

Dr. Valerie D. W. James

Chief Leadership, Learning and Efficiency Officer VisionSpot Consulting Group

What people have to say about Tavis Banks…

"His passion and energy is contagious. He is always ready to develop programs and ideas that can better serve our teams. His flexibility and grit is outstanding, always giving feedback and recommendations. It is and has been a pleasure to work with him."

– Ilan Shapiro, MD Physician at AltaMed Health Services

"I remembered the concepts from your training class, how much fun it was and what an impact you made on my moving forward in the company."

– Julia H. Project Manager at Optum Rx

"Working with Tavis for 2 years was a blessing. He kept me motivated on a daily basis and always brought a smile to the job. He is a dedicated individual with a heart of gold. He is amazing!"

– Christina Kruger – Business Operations Specialist

"Tavis was very supportive with all staff members and served as a sponsor for many including myself. Tavis motivated those around him and served as an excellent leader and mentor."

– Aregenis Ruvalcaba, Resident Advisor Supervisor at UC Irvine School of Medicine

T3

Train the Trainer

*10 Things Every Successful Trainer **Must Know***

Tavis A. Banks

Copyright 2019 by Tavis A. Banks

All rights reserved. No part of this publication may be reproduced, distributed, or transmitted in any form or by any means, including photocopying, recording, or other electronic or mechanical methods, without the prior written permission of the publisher, except in the case of brief quotations embodied in critical reviews and other non-commercial uses permitted by copyright law.

First printing, 2019

Printed in the United States of America

Avant Garde Training Group

ISBN: 9781672828826

This book is dedicated to:

My four sons, who taught me that life is a never-ending cycle of learning, training, teaching and constant adjustment

Also, to those who allowed me to lead them throughout my career and pushed me to grow as a **leader**

T3

Train the Trainer

10 Things Every Successful Trainer **Must Know**

CONTENTS

FOREWORD xvi

INTRODUCTION 1

HOW I GOT STARTED IN TRAINING AND WHY I WROTE THIS BOOK 1

CHAPTER 1 11

OPENING THE CLASS: INTRODUCTIONS, ICE-BREAKERS, AND ENERGIZERS 11

    Types of Introductions 13

        Verbal Introduction 13

        Introduction and Informational Slides 13

        Personal Introduction Slide 14

        Class Informational Slide 15

        Ground Rules and Housekeeping 16

    Ice-Breakers 17

    Introduce the topic and give them the Why? - WIIFM 27

    Don't Just Jump into The Steps 29

    Always Have an Agenda 32

CHAPTER 2 35
KNOW YOUR STUDENTS LEARNING STYLES 35

Types of Learners and Learning Styles 36

For Visual Learners Use Visual Aids 37

    Easel Charts or Dry Erase Boards 39

    Training Videos 40

    Props 41

For Auditory Learners Use Lectures, Sound Bites and Speaking Opportunities 42

    Example One: Pre-Recorded Calls 43

    Example Two: Live Call Listening 44

For Kinesthetic Learners, Let Them Do It 46

CHAPTER 3 49
MAKE LEARNING FUN 49

Learning Activities 50

Educational Games (Activities) 51

Computer Simulated Activities 53

The Fish Philosophy 55

CHAPTER 4 59
SOFT SKILLS 59

Soft Skills 60

Customer Service 61

Connect with the Class 63

Relate to the Learners 64

Use Real Life Stories 65

CHAPTER 5 67

- CLASS MANAGEMENT 67
  - Time and Attendance 68
  - Work the Room 69
  - Utilize your Spare Time 70
  - Encourage Class Participation 72
  - Use Incentives, Give-Aways, and Prizes 73
  - Have a Ringer in the Audience! 74

CHAPTER 6 77
- **FACILITATION TECHNIQUES AND MORE** 77
  - Facilitation Styles 78
    - Lectures 78
    - Breakout Sessions 79
    - Question and Answer or Q&A Sessions 80
    - Training Videos 81
    - Teach-Backs 81
    - The Toss-Back Method 82
    - Live Training Examples 84
    - OJT or On the Job Training 86
  - Periodically Check/Test for Understanding and Retention 87
  - Show Em, Don't Tell Em! 89
  - Do Not Give Them Everything, Teach Them to Fish 89
  - Do They Know Where to Find It? 90

CHAPTER 7 93
- **WRITING AND DESIGNING TRAINING MATERIAL** 93
  - Instructional Design 97
  - Break It Up! /Chunking 98

    Activities 99

    Case Studies 100

    Creating an Agenda 103

    Creating a Trainer's Syllabus 104

CHAPTER 8 107

TESTS OR REVIEWS FOR UNDERSTANDING 107

    Tests/Quizzes for Understanding 108

    Reviews for Understanding 111

        Straight Review Activity 111

        A-Z Activity 113

        Teach-Back Review Activity 115

        Educational Games (Activities) 115

    What Did You Learn? (Yesterday, This Morning, This Afternoon) *Activity* 116

    Is More Review Needed? 117

        Call Confirmation Review 118

CHAPTER 9 121

SUPER USERS, E-LEARNING, AND SELF-PACED LEARNING 121

    Super Users 122

    E-Learning 123

    Live Online Training Sessions 124

    Self-Paced Online Courses (LMS Courses) 126

    Pre-Recorded Online Training Sessions 130

    Read and Confirm (Attestations) 131

CHAPTER 10 133

CLOSING THE CLASS 133

Final Reviews and Quizzes 134

Contact Information 135

Thank the Participants for Coming 137

EPILOGUE: 139

DID I ANSWER ALL OF YOUR QUESTIONS?.. 139

What do I do with difficult participants like Know It All's? 140

How do I handle people in the class who know more than I do about the subject matter? 141

What do I do if I don't know the answer to the question I'm being asked? 143

How do I stay on track in the classroom?.. 147

What is a Trainer's Toolkit, and what are the things that go into it? 150

What should I do with participants who arrive late? 151

How do I handle situations when the equipment has technical issues? 152

References.. 158

Acknowledgments

Thank you to my wife for supporting me during the writing of this book, which has definitely been a journey. Your encouragement, words of wisdom, and drive to push me to pursue my passion fueled me to complete this project.

I want to acknowledge the leaders who mentored me from the past, present, and current, whether they were aware or not they were mentoring me at the time.

Much thanks to my children who have been and will continue to be a constant source of lessons learned.

There is an opportunity to learn lessons from any experience, situation, problem, or triumph. The key is to keep learning.

FOREWORD
HOW DID I GET HERE?

Hi, my name is Tavis Banks, and I'd like to tell you how I got involved with training. I've worked in the healthcare industry for over 20 years. The last 15 years of that time has been spent working in Training and Development. I wish I could tell you that I knew as a young boy that I always wanted to be an educator, but that is not the case. Honestly, I stumbled into training. I found my passion because I was bored, which in turn led to me becoming **passionate** about Training and Development. I believe this is essential to point out because we all don't always have things figured out when we are young adults. Though we may not start out knowing exactly who we want to become, this doesn't mean we can't figure it out. Sometimes it takes diving into one thing to learn; we want to do something else.

My career began in the healthcare field as a Pharmacy Technician in 1994, pretty much right out of high school. At the time, I chose not to attend a traditional college or the military, so my mom being my mom, took me for a ride. She stopped in front of a Technical College in Long Beach, CA. She said, "You are going to pick a program. Whatever financial aid doesn't cover, I'll help you with." That's how I became a Pharmacy Technician and started my career. Shortly after a three-month internship in a hospital I was hired for my first official job as a Pharmacy Technician at a large retail chain store, Sav-On Pharmacy..

Sav-On Pharmacy was a significant player during that time. I made great relationships and started to hone my customer service skills there. It was a very busy pharmacy at the time. We regularly filled over 1000 prescriptions per day, (sometimes 1500!) which was a lot back then, especially when you were counting medication by hand. There were a few employees that worked there for years, but the majority were newbies like me. We had a bit of turnover, which meant opportunities to show new people how things worked at the pharmacy. Working here was my first real introduction to training other people. I worked at Sav-On for two years before I moved on. When it was all said and done, I worked retail, hospital, mail order, home health, and in drug re-packaging., you name it, I pretty much did it. I made my rounds through the pharmaceutical industry, stopping short of becoming a Pharmaceutical Drug Rep. Eventually, I ended up working for a Pharmacy Benefit Manager (PBM) called Prescription Solutions in Costa Mesa, CA. Prescription Solutions was later bought out by UnitedHealth Group, who eventually changed the name of the PBM to Optum Rx. At prescription Solutions, I worked in the Call Center (now referred to as Contact Centers) on the Pharmacy Help Desk assisting pharmacies with member eligibility, processing prescription claims, and in the Mail Services Department processing mail-order prescriptions. I was able to meet many new people and had tons of fun.

So, what does all the information I just gave you have to do with training?

It is all a part of what made me well...me. All these moments were learning experiences that I used later on in my career. These events prepared me for my life as a trainer, leader, and speaker. I even helped to start the official Contact Center training department while at UnitedHealth Group, which gave me a great sense of accomplishment.

When I graduated high school, I had no idea what I wanted to do with my life. I was looking to go to school part-time and get a job. I couldn't have imagined I would end up with a career I loved in Education, Training, and Leadership Development.

So now that you know a little about my story let's get into the reason I wrote this book, my love of Training!

T3

INTRODUCTION
HOW I GOT STARTED IN TRAINING AND WHY I WROTE THIS BOOK

Working in a Contact Center for a large healthcare company allowed me the opportunity to learn a myriad of things about myself:

- It was easy for me to speak to customers.
- I became bored very quickly taking phone calls.
- I liked customer service.
- I needed more purpose in my work life.
- I needed to get off those phones!

Prescription Solutions hired me as a Pharmacy Technician in a Customer Service Agent role. It did not take long before I realized this was not my dream job. I was taking calls for about a couple of months before I decided I had to do something about my situation. I wanted to get off of those phones badly! One day, I asked my supervisor if there was anything else I could do for her. Surely, she had some work I could take off her plate. Being proactive led me to responsibility for resolving escalated calls, assisting with special projects, and helping others inside and outside of my department. One of those special projects was sitting in new hire training classes as a Subject Matter Expert (SME) to assist the primary trainer. I started my training career just helping out in classes and had a lot of fun doing so. I soon discovered I had found a passion. The business model at the time was to send everyone who was hired in the call center through New Hire Customer Service Training, regardless of their position. Going through the entire training would give everyone an appreciation for the department and connect them to the mission. This created a lasting impression on the new hires. As trainers, we were the first introduction to newly hired employees at the company. I was able to meet tons of new people, which I really enjoyed! The best part of it all was, I was off the phones! Honestly, I fell in love with training and loved the feeling educating people gave me. I know it sounds corny, but when someone is struggling with learning a new task, seeing that light bulb moment when they finally get it makes me happy. Fortunately for me, I was paired up with a trainer that preferred not to do certain things. Everything they didn't want to do I did, and while doing so, I was able to gain lots of experience. Another thing about the trainer was they did not like confrontation and habitually avoided it. Since my trainer was afraid to have conversations about discipline with people, I took on that activity as well.

Handling confrontation was a skill I was always comfortable with. I considered myself to be a leader and operated as such. After they saw I was good at it, I began conducting all the disciplinary meetings for my trainer. If someone had an attendance issue, I would have those conversations with the trainee. If someone had an attitude problem, I handled it. I was resolving issues, which I loved, and my trainer appreciated. Back in my early days with the company, we had an in-house temp agency, so the trainers assumed a level of responsibility for recommendations on hiring and firing. Even though the agency facilitated the actual sourcing and releasing of candidates, the trainers often made the decisions on who the call center retained or released. I formed relationships with the staffing agency folks and pretty soon I had the responsibility and autonomy to determine who was going to be a good fit for the organization. That gave me a great sense of pride and duty to ensure I was training and mentoring the success of the new staff. After all, my name would be attached to those employees moving forward, and I did not want to disappoint them, my leadership, or myself.

I think what made me a little different from my peers is I the way in which my mind processed information. Because I hold a Ph.D. in Common Sense, everything I do starts with the question, *"Does this make sense?"* For me, even the most complex projects start with that simple question. I need to understand or at least get a good grasp of what is going on and why the person is requesting training before I jump to a solution. Many people provide solutions to problems before they even know what the issue is, and that often leads to

"Training is a huge responsibility and, in some organizations, can be a multi-million-dollar investment."

miscommunication and re-work. (Which I hate doing.) In addition to my Ph.D. in Common Sense, I earned a Bachelor's degree and a Master's Degree in Management from Baker University in Baldwin City, Kansas and from the University of Redlands in Redlands, California, respectively (Go Bulldogs!) I have been passionately working in Training and Development since 2004 (15 years) and have a long history of questioning everyone and everything from my brother, my parents, authority figures, and myself! (Just ask my parents and they will tell you.) I love a good debate and getting to the root cause of problems and issues to ensure we are matching the correct solution to the right problem. Now that we have my qualifications out of the way let's get on with why you are reading this book.

You are reading this book because you are either:

- New to the field of training
- Not new to training but are looking for some common-sense approaches and even some tips and tricks to help you facilitate your training sessions more effectively.

I want to give you the foundation every trainer needs to build the most successful training career, organization, or empire. My goal is for you to understand that all trainers who have become great trainers have been exactly where you are now. They learned techniques to propel them to become better trainers and towards training mastery. Training is a huge responsibility and, in some organizations, can be a multi-million-dollar investment. In fact, according to Training Industry.com, it is estimated that over 366 Billion dollars was spent on training globally in 2018. Training is often one of the first real points of contact a new employee has with the organization. It is an opportunity to form and mold new-hires and their experience with the company. I would like for you to understand, training does not have to be so intimidating. In this book, I will give you some common-sense approaches to learning and development for you and your staff. Similar to the different styles in your wardrobes throughout the '80s, '90s or 2000s, training has many different looks. Training does not have to be the instructor standing in front of a room full of people lecturing to them while the audience is disengaged or falling asleep. When conducted properly, training can be an action-packed, fun-filled, experience and can lead to a rewarding career.

Now it's time for a pop quiz! Yup, you heard me, a pop quiz!

Don't worry, it won't be that difficult, and I will only ask you two questions.

> ***Question 1:*** *How do you eat an elephant?*
> ***Answer****: One bite at a time.*

How does this relate to training? Many training classes tackle a large amount of information, and you cannot give everything to the learners all at once. That would be like giving them a drink of water from a firehose! You want to deliver the information to the participants in baby steps, bits, pieces, or chunks. The key is to distribute large amounts of content to your learners without overwhelming them. So, everyone, get your virtual knife and fork and eat that elephant one bite at a time!

I realize some of you don't eat meat and may have been offended by my last question, but for those of you still with me, I promise no animals were harmed or consumed in the making of this book. It is just a figure of speech. Let's move on.

> ***Question 2****: Is training an art or a science?*

Answer*: It is a little bit of both.*

The philosophies behind how and why we train a certain way and how we get adult learners to retain information is a science. The style in which we do it is an art-form. In her book, **The Art and Science of Training,** Elaine Biech explains, "Science is both a body of knowledge and a process. Art is the expression of creativity and imagination." Biech describes how learning and development are scientific, and also highlights that *"training success lies in knowing what to do when things don't go as planned."* This statement emphasizes the artistry of training and is the best of both worlds for me. I love to be creative but also celebrate the necessity of facts and data, so when you combine the two, it is like magic.

One of my responsibilities as a Training Manager is to recruit and hire staff. Various positions include Training Coordinators, Training Specialists and Instructional Designers. In my current department, the perfect Training Specialist would have the following attributes:

- Prior training experience
- Experience in a healthcare setting
- Experience as a Medical Assistant or Licensed Vocational Nurse
- Excellent customer service skills
- College graduate or equivalent experience

Depending on your industry, you will develop your own set of skills relevant to the position in which you are hired or hiring for. Usually, these attributes would be listed in the job description; however, they are not always there. You must inform the recruiter which qualities are most imperative, and which are non-negotiable. These qualities should be included in the updated job description, so you don't waste your, the recruiter's, or the candidate's time. I don't always find candidates with all the preferred attributes or skills, but that does not disqualify a candidate for me. Many times, I am not able to source that "perfect" candidate. As a result, I must develop the employee after they have accepted the offer of employment. Many people interview well but are not able to hold up the end of the bargain when it is time to perform. Because of this, I give new trainers a 90-day trial period. During this

"Training is not solely the instructor standing in front of a room full of people lecturing to them while the audience is disengaged or falling asleep."

time, I have my mentors assess the skills of the new team member and give them pointers and feedback to prepare them for training classes on their own. Before the 90-day evaluation, I meet with the mentors and the mentee. As I conducted one-on-one meetings and feedback sessions, the trainers and mentors started to ask me for advice on how to handle multiple situations. They asked me what they should do if a trainee arrived late, if someone needed special accommodations, how to overcome nervousness, and how to facilitate various types of training. There were questions regarding how to best teach Technical Training, Soft Skills, New Hire Training, Refresher Training, 1:1 Training, and Online Trainings. They all require a different set of skills to be able to facilitate them successfully, and my trainers had plenty of questions about each. All these questions prompted me to develop a training course on things new trainers should know. This would be a skill-builder Training 101 course which I call a T3 or Train the Trainer. I wanted to make sure everyone was on the same page. I was excited to do so because it took me back to my core as a trainer and I was able to showcase the knowledge that I have gained over the years. It also allowed me to facilitate a class, which I did not get the opportunity to do very often at the time.

In preparation for the skill-builder session, I sent out a survey to the team asking which topics they wanted to review or in which situations they were having difficulty. Once I gathered all the information, I started to build the class. I was very eager to impart my wisdom of training techniques and share my common-sense approach. I also wanted to learn from the trainers and get their perspectives on various situations. I am a leader that knows you can learn from your staff, understanding that everyone has different experiences which provide varying viewpoints. The newer trainers seemed a little skeptical because they had never seen me in action, and I was anxious to show them what I could do. This would be the first test for me as their new leader, and my team did not disappoint. The survey elicited additional questions like:

- What should I do with late or difficult participants?
- How do I handle situations when the equipment has technical issues?

- What do I do if I don't know the answer to the question the trainees have?
- What if the people in the class know more than I do about the subject matter than I do? (Yes, that can happen.)

I was excited. These were all great questions. I couldn't wait to get in front of my team to share the experiences I have had over the years and develop my trainers' skills. My group had a thirst for knowledge, and I had answers that would help them learn, grow, and develop them into better trainers. We would embark on a journey that I hoped would change their careers and set them on the path to training and leadership excellence. I told them, if they chose to stay focused and dedicated, this could change their lives.

As the great W.E.B. DuBois said, "Education must not simply teach work – it must teach Life."

CHAPTER 1
OPENING THE CLASS: INTRODUCTIONS, ICE-BREAKERS, AND ENERGIZERS

Question: How should I start my classes?

Answer: You open the class by getting to know the participants with activities full of energy, excitement, and fun!

This chapter contains information on the following topics:

- **Types of Introductions**
    - Verbal Introductions
    - Introduction and Informational Slides
    - Personal Introduction Slide
    - Class Informational Slide
    - Ground Rules and Housekeeping
- **Ice Breakers**
- **Introduce the topic and give them the Why? - WIIFM**
- **Don't Just Jump into The Steps**
- **Create an Agenda**

"The key to growth is the introduction of high dimensions of consciousness into our awareness." – Lao Tzu

It is critical to do three things when starting a class:

- Introduce yourself and the class to each other!
- Break the ice!
- Inject some life to the class!

Doing these three things will set the tone for your entire training. Not only must **you** have high energy, but you must also be able to transfer that energy to your audience. When facilitating classes, I always tell my audience that I feed off their energy. This means I give them a level of responsibility as to how the session will go. If my audience gives off low energy, I will have low energy. If they radiate a high amount of energy, then I will exude a great deal of energy. I learned over the years, I must be excited from the start, but it is true to some extent that I feed off my audiences' energy and participation. The more excitement I can create, the more they get involved in the session, and in turn, I become more dynamic. It is a cycle that feeds into the law of attraction; you attract what you put out! Remember, when you are opening a class, you must:

"Not only must you have high energy, you must be able to transfer that energy to your audience."

- Introduce yourself
- Allow the participants to introduce themselves
- Take care of housekeeping
- Conduct an effective ice-breaker and keep the room energized!

Let's dive into some ways to accomplish all three tasks.

Types of Introductions

Verbal Introduction

A verbal introduction is probably the most common, and it is very straightforward. Stand in front of your audience and introduce yourself to the learners. Give your class some background information about you. Start building a relationship and some rapport by letting them know a little bit more about you. Your qualifications for training the course, where you went to school, how long you've been with the organization, things like that. They should already have a general understanding of the class but give them a description of the class and why they want to be there (Remember the term WIFFM discussed later in the book.) Doing this lets the audience know what to expect during the training. A good practice is to tell the participants how long the class is, what time the breaks are, and where the restrooms are located.

Introduction and Informational Slides

Informational and Introduction slides can be beneficial when used correctly. Depending on the type of class and the duration, you may use different types of introduction slides. These slides can serve as an introduction, give background information on you, or provide general information about the class. They can also take care of some of the administrative tasks, like displaying the agenda and schedule for the day. I've even used informational slides as break timers to let people know how much time is left on the break while displaying questions and answers relating to the class on the screen.

Personal Introduction Slide

A Personal Introduction slide will share some personal things about yourself (likes, dislikes, hobbies, etc.) If you are conducting a 30-minute Technical Training, you probably do not want to use this type of introduction slide. Letting the class know about all of your personal interests will take too long. If you ask the entire class to share the same information, your course will be over before you get an opportunity to get into the content. Some of the information in a Personal Introduction slide could include the following:

- Your name
- Experience (Length of time in the company and industry)
- Qualifications (Degrees, certifications)
- Favorite food, color, book, quote or expression
- A fun fact about yourself
- Hobbies

Figure 1.1 Example of a Personal Introduction Slide

Class Informational Slide

This type of introduction slide will present information about the class that can be useful to the participants. It can ensure they are in the correct room, give information about the presenter, or cover the ground rules.

The information listed on the Class information slide could include the following:

- Name or Title of the course
- Time and dates for the course
- Trainer's name
- Trainer's contact information (Email, phone number, website address)

Figure 1.2 Example of Class Information Slide

Ground Rules and Housekeeping

Establishing ground rules is one exercise that often gets overlooked but can be an integral part of your training classes. It is essential to include this step upfront because it could save you time and headaches later.

The **Ground Rules Informational Slide** will contain important housekeeping information. The length or duration of the class will determine how I handle the ground rules. If the course is short, I will display a pre-created slide with commonly accepted ground rules. If the class is two days or longer, I will facilitate an exercise that allows the class to create their own ground rules. People who are involved in the process of developing the rules tend to be more willing to follow them. I, or one of the participants in the class, will record the rules on a piece of easel chart paper and post them to the wall for everyone to see. Don't worry if the class doesn't include all of the necessary ground rules, you can add any remaining rules to the list before it is complete. Usually, the participants get most of them, and there are only a couple of items that need to be added to the list.

> *"Establishing ground rules is one exercise that gets overlooked many times but can be an integral part of your training classes."*

You may ask, "What if I want to display multiple slides?" Well, that is simple. You can set the slides to display with a timer and have them repeat. This is the slideshow function of PowerPoint. This way, the audience sees the information multiple times, can write the information down, or take pictures of the information on their cell phones like most of us do now. Music can also be added to the presentation slide(s) to enhance the experience. Soft Jazz creates a calming mood. Upbeat or happy songs make people feel good about the information they are going to receive. Hard Rock songs get people pumped up about the session! These have all worked well for me in training classes.

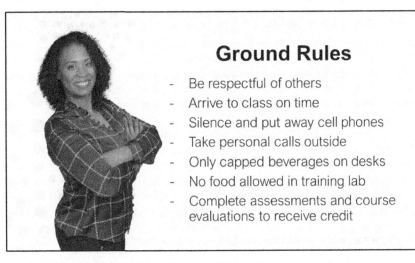

Figure 1.3 Example of Ground Rules Information Slide

Ice-Breakers

I love icebreakers. Icebreakers are always a great introduction to the course, no matter the time of day. Icebreakers are an excellent opportunity to meet trainees. They can allow you to get to know your trainees better or guide them into an activity that you want them to do later. They can be fun, and though they can be directly related to the subject matter, they do not always have to be. If you decide to make them related to the subject matter, they can also be used to review what you learned the day before or that morning. Some icebreakers even allow the participants to use critical thinking and teamwork.

Conducting an effective ice-breaker will keep the room energized and everyone involved. Ice-Breakers are great tools to:

- Loosen up the participants and ease tension and nervousness amongst the learners
- Prepare the class or get them ready to learn for the day or afternoon
- Give the class a mental break when learning very dense material
- Serve as a precursory exercise to the learning ahead
- Serve as a review session for the group
- Re-direct learners if there are technical difficulties during the session

Icebreakers can also be used to connect people who would not typically work together in a group to create bonding or form new relationships. In this book, I've included a few of my favorite icebreakers that I have learned over the years and instructions on how to use them.

1. Simple Elevator Introduction Ice-Breaker

Small or Large Group Activity

Time Needed: 10-15 mins

You Will Need:

- Group leader or facilitator
- Instructions slide
- Wall Charts and Markers (Optional)

Overview/Objective:

The Simple Elevator Introduction ice-breaker is simple and seeks to gain basic information about the participants in the class. Examples of questions included in a simple introduction ice-breaker are:

- Tell us your name?
- What is your business background? (What company or industry did you work prior?)
- What are your hobbies?
- What are your pet peeves?
- What was your first job?
- What is your favorite color?
- What was your first car, or which kind of car did you drive in high school?
- Did you or do you currently play any sports? If so, which one(s)?

These are all simple questions that everyone can answer and work well for this exercise. Simple Introduction Slides allow people to share basic facts about them themselves and gives them a chance to find things in common.

Instructions:

Verbally give the participants the questions, display them written on a wall chart or a PowerPoint slide for this exercise. Any of these methods will work. But beware, if you only ask the questions verbally without a visual in a large class, the participants may forget the questions, and you will end up repeating the questions quite often. However, this can show you which learners in the class are auditory learners or who can learn things quickly. (Remember, there are learning opportunities everywhere.)

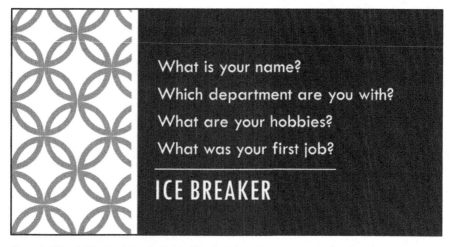

Figure 1.4 Simple Elevator Introduction Ice Breaker

2. Name Tent/Card Introduction Ice-Breaker

Small or Large Group Activity

Time Needed: 10-15 mins

You Will Need:

- Group leader or facilitator
- Instructions slide
- Name Tag Cards or an 8.5" x 11" Sheet of paper (One sheet per person)
- Markers or colored pencils for the participants

Overview/Objective

The Name Tent/Card Introduction ice-breaker is a fun exercise that has the participants to introduce themselves creatively. The drawings are always fun and provide a chance to find out who are the artists in the room and who is artistically challenged. The information gained in this exercise can be useful later if you facilitate an activity that involves drawing or you need a volunteer during the course. The more outgoing people will usually self-identify during this ice-breaker. This exercise will provide insights about the learners like what motivates them, their likes, dislikes and which topics you as the facilitator can discuss to relate to them.

Instructions:

In the Name Tag Introduction Ice Breaker, the facilitator will pass out markers to the participants. Everyone will write or draw their name, title, and something that represents something they love or love to do.

It can be a hobby or something like music or favorite food. After everyone has completed their name tags, have them explain the meanings behind the drawings. You, as the facilitator, should join in the fun and create a name tent/card as well.

Figure 1.5 Name Tent/Tag Introduction Ice Breaker

3. Two Truths and a Lie Ice-Breaker

Small or Large Group Activity

Time Needed: 10-15 mins

You Will Need:

- Group leader or facilitator
- Instructions Slide
- 3x5 Index Cards (One card per person)
- Ink pens or pencils for the participants

Overview/Objective

The Two Truths and a Lie ice-breaker is a classic. This ice-breaker exercise positions the group to learn more about each other that you wouldn't necessarily find out in a casual conversation. It can be a team-building/bonding experience, and people can find out things about each other they have in common.

Instructions:

 Participants write two true statements about themselves and one statement that is not true on a 3x5 card. The amount of time allotted will determine how you facilitate the exercise. If there is enough time, the facilitator can collect the cards and read each one aloud while participants try and guess who the card is describing, which statements are correct, and which is the lie. If there is a limited amount of time, the participants can read their own card while the group tries to figure out which statements are true, and which is the lie. This ice-breaker works any time of the day, is sure to be a hit, and will energize the class. It often uncovers fascinating facts about the participants.

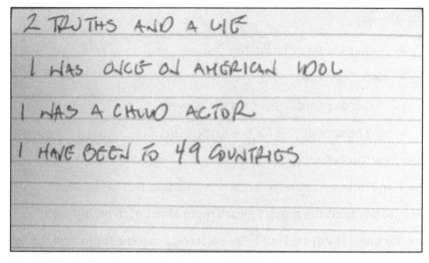

Figure 1.6 Two Truths and a Lie Ice-Breaker Example 3x5 Card

4. Never Have I Ever Ice-Breaker

Small or Large Group Activity

Time Needed: 10-15 mins

You Will Need:

- Group leader or facilitator
- Instructions Slide
- Never Have I Ever presentation or list of questions on paper
- Never Have I Ever double-sided paddle (One paddle per person)

Overview/Objective

The Never Have I Ever ice-breaker is one that you may be familiar with as it is a popular party game. This ice-breaker exercise positions the group to learn more about each other and can be a team-building/bonding experience. People tend to quickly find out things about each other they have in common.

Instructions:

Give each participant a Never Have I Ever Paddle. Begin the ice-breaker by asking the questions from the Never Have I Ever list of questions. Participants will answer questions by holding up their paddle with either the **I Have** or **Never Have I** side facing forward. Everyone will be able to see how each other answered, and you, as the facilitator can ask follow-up questions to participants at random.

Figure 1.7 Never Have I Ever Paddles

Introduce the topic and give them the Why? - WIIFM

Early in my training career, I attended a meeting about an upcoming project with several department leaders. I guess I asked too many questions; because the supervisor leading the session (Let's call him Cary) stopped and asked me, "Do you listen to WIIFM Radio station?" I asked, "What's that?" Cary said, you know, WIIFM, What's In It For Me? It's when people care more about what they're going to get out of it than what they are putting in." He meant it to be a derogatory statement and intended to silence me, but boy was he wrong. Cary, the supervisor, did not truly understand the magnitude of the reference he was using. I replied, "Yes! I keep my radio tuned to that station because I want to stay informed in everything I do." I feel it's crucial to inform people of what they are getting into. I didn't understand how you could tell someone to do something without giving them the context behind it. It's like someone telling you to run into a burning building and not ask any questions, just do it. Um, no, that's not me. You have to explain to me why I'm running into the burning building. It doesn't have to be a long drawn out story, but I need to know some key details:

- Am I rushing in to save a baby?
- Am I going in to save someone's stuffed animal collection?
- Am I running into the building because the person telling me to do so does not want me to come back out?

These are all things that run through my mind when someone tells me I need to do something and don't worry, it's okay, trust me. Nope! I am a processor; I analyze things. Sometimes I jump to the wrong conclusion or automatically go to the worst-case scenario, but that's just how I think. It is how my brain is wired. Other people think differently, and that's alright. However, I believe that people do a better job if they understand why they're doing what they're doing.

"I feel it's very important to inform people of what they are getting into. I didn't understand how you could tell someone to do something without giving them the context behind it."

I fully understand, if my name is not on the side of the building (meaning if I do not own the company), I cannot always do what I want to do. Quite frankly, I may not even get the answers to the questions I have. I may not have full autonomy regarding all the decisions I make at work. However, most people want a return on their investment; and I am no exception if I am investing my time, energy, and efforts. When people understand what's in it for them and why they're doing what they are doing, they are more willing to care about it, make fewer mistakes or take fewer shortcuts. If you can get them to believe in the mission or the "Why" behind it (the What's In It For Them), they will give you all they have and then some to achieve the goal.

Don't Just Jump into The Steps

Another reason why you should introduce the topic and give people the why is the introduction itself can serve as an icebreaker. Give them the WIIFM! It gives people a chance to understand what they're about to get into; this way, they are prepared and know what's in it for them. One day I was sitting in on one of my trainers Technical Training classes bright and early on a Monday morning. The trainer greeted the trainees, sat them down, instructed them to look at the screen up front, and proceeded to jump into the steps. I thought, "Wow, no introduction, no agenda, no review of what they were going to do? Immediately go into Step One, yikes!" As I jotted down some notes I'd use for feedback for the trainer; I looked around the room. Some of the trainees seemed bothered as if they were caught off-guard, but they just went with it. During the break, I asked the trainer if they thought it was a good idea to jump right into the steps without facilitating an icebreaker or explaining to people what they were going to be doing. (I always use these types of situations as learning opportunities and use questions rather than punishing statements up front to give the trainers a chance to discover their own improvement opportunities and solutions.) The trainer responded to me by saying, "Oh, I was saving the icebreaker until after the break." I replied to the trainer, "That's one way to facilitate, good luck, you're going to need it." They asked what I meant, so I explained to the trainer. "By not properly

> *"Give them the WIIFM! It gives people a chance to understand what they're about to get into, this way they are prepared and know what's in it for them."*

introducing the class and giving explanatory instructions this morning, it seems you have mentally lost some of your people already. You will have to work that much harder to gain back their confidence and trust." While you can facilitate icebreakers after a break; they most certainly should be conducted at the beginning of a class. Especially a new hire training class, because it sets the tone for the course. There is no hard and fast rule that states you cannot do more than one ice-breaker during a training session. Even if your ice-breaker is a simple exercise that introduces you to the class, you should still conduct one. It doesn't have to take a long time, it may only last a few minutes, but those few minutes will save you time and unnecessary questions in the long run. Because of that experience in the classroom that day, I made some changes with our facilitation practices and the team implemented:

1. An introduction slide that would serve as a high level informational
2. Mandatory icebreakers for every trainer at the beginning of every class
3. Quarterly evaluation/review sessions with the trainers conducted by me, a supervisor or the leads

The informational slide made sure the participants knew why they were there. This comes in handy, especially when you have multiple classes running at the same time. It allows people to see if they are in the correct class quickly. The mandatory ice-breaker ensured the beginning of each class started with an energizing exercise to set the mood for the class! The quarterly evaluation/review sessions allowed regular feedback for the trainers, and to specifically address their facilitation skills and in-class performance. My team and I came up with a Trainer Feedback Form to allow for structured criticism that would be fair and included industry best practices and key performance indicators. I purposely excluded any scoring values, so the exercise would be purely feedback on what went well during the class and where there was an opportunity for improvement. The trainers appreciated that because they were not focused on a grade or a score and allowed them to accept the feedback better.

Figure 1.8 Class Introduction Slide Example

Always Have an Agenda

What is an agenda? An agenda will explain and highlight the key topics covered during the training session. Your agenda is like your roadmap. It lets the participants know where **you** will be going during the training session and can even be used to keep you on track. The agenda gives the participants an idea of how the class is organized and can be displayed in some of the following ways:

- On a PowerPoint slide
- On easel chart paper
- You can give them a printed paper copy

Keep in mind there are different types of agendas and they can be used for various purposes. High-level agendas provide a list of topics covered, and detailed-agendas give more information on the subjects discussed during the class. Depending on the type of course, after introducing myself and presenting the agenda, I'd sometimes ask the participants, "What would you like to get out of this session, or what would you like to learn during this course?" Then I would record their responses on a sheet of easel chart paper. Most of the time, the topics the participants presented would fit in somewhere later in the class content anyway. As I facilitate the class, I make sure to check the topics off the list. Weaving their topics into the session is very important. It helps to gain the participants' buy-in, ensure they get

"Making sure to weave their topics into the session is very important.

This helps to gain the participants buy-in, ensure they get something of value they want out of the class and boosts your credibility."

something of value they want out of the class, and boost your credibility. If any topics remained uncovered during the lesson, I made sure to address them before the session ended, usually during the end of a section or at the end of the day review.

Figure 1.9 High-Level Agenda Slide

CHAPTER 2
KNOW YOUR STUDENTS LEARNING STYLES

Question: Why do we use different methods of teaching? Can't we just train everyone the same way?

Answer: We styles use different training styles because people are different. Not everyone learns the same way, and we want to make sure we use a variety of learning styles to capture all the participants' attention.

This chapter contains information on the following topics:

- **Types of Learners and Learning Styles**
- **For Visual Learners use Visual Aids**
    - PowerPoint Presentations
    - Easel Charts and Dry Erase Boards
    - Training Videos
    - Props
- **For Auditory Learners use Lectures, Sound Bites, and Speaking Opportunities**
    - Pre-Recorded Calls/Live Call Listening
- **For Kinesthetic Learners, Let Them Do It**

"For the things we have to learn before we can do them, we learn by doing them." – Aristotle

Types of Learners and Learning Styles

What do you think about when you read the term Learning Styles? Do you think about how you prefer to take in information? Maybe you like to read books; perhaps you prefer to listen to audiobooks, or maybe you like to do things hands-on and figure it out yourself. Think about how you have learned to do something in the past. Were you taught how to do it by someone? Were you given a set of instructions and followed those instructions? Let me give you a more specific example.

The Infamous Bookcase

Have you ever bought something like a bookcase and had to put it together yourself? If so, did you:

a. Layout all of the pieces in order and carefully read the instructions.

b. Go onto YouTube and watch a video on how to put together the bookcase and followed along.

c. Chucked those instructions and just figured out to do it on your own. (*Then wondered why you had extra pieces at the end and said HA! Who needs them!*)

In your classes, there will be students with different learning styles. If you stick to just one form of facilitation or learning style, you will be doing yourself and your audience a great disservice. Because you may not be able to cater to each participant or conduct one-on-one style training, you must recognize this when you are designing and facilitating your training courses. Part of your pre-work for the class will be to make sure to include the various learning styles. According to an article written on MindTools.com Psychologists in the 1920s developed a learning model called the VAK Model. This model consisted of three main learning styles and has been recognized in the learning and training industry for almost 100 years as the most common ways people prefer to learn. The three learning styles are:

- Visual – Learn by seeing
- Auditory – Learn by hearing
- Kinesthetic – Learn by doing

Again, there will most likely be all three types of learners in your class, so don't just use one style, mix it up a bit.

For Visual Learners Use Visual Aids

PowerPoint presentations are the most common method of visual aids during training sessions and used in different ways. While they are frequently overused, PowerPoints can be helpful. How and when you use PowerPoint presentations (or not) will depend on the size of your audience, method of training, and if the training is more interactive.

"In your classes there will be students with different learning styles. If you stick to just one style of facilitation or learning style you will be doing yourself and your audience a great disservice."

A general rule regarding PowerPoints is they should be used as a tool to enhance your training, not as the sole form of presentation or your only training source. The slides should not be full of text. There are a few different rules of thumb like the 5x5, 6x6 or even the 7x7 method, where it is suggested the user limit the number of words per line and bullet points per slide. These rules are employed to ensure the slides are not overly packed with text. If so, people will make a choice to pay attention to either the slide or you. Presumably, because of this issue, there was a style of PowerPoint presentation created that does not use text at all called Pecha Kucha. Pecha Kucha originated in Japan and uses 20 slides shown for 20 seconds each and contains only pictures. You must be on top of your game with this presentation style. I prescribe plenty of practice to make sure your timing is correct before attempting this one in front of an audience. If I see someone with a presentation full of text, it tells me a couple of things:

1. The facilitator is not familiar with their material, and they are using the slides as a crutch
2. They need a training manual.

Figure 2.1 Typical PowerPoint Slide to Enhance Lecture

Easel Charts or Dry Erase Boards

One of my favorite visual aids I use in classes are **Easel Charts** or **Dry Erase Boards**. They are a great way to break up the monotony and even get people involved. I like these because you can use them for multiple reasons:

- Have preprinted information like Ground Rules displayed
- Pose a question to the group and record answers real-time
- Have the participants get involved in the action by getting out of their seats and writing information down on the charts
- Use charts as a "Parking Lot" for questions to be answered at a later time
- Use them as part of a review session to be referred to later during the class

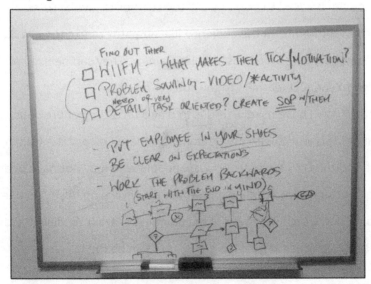

Figure 2.2 Dry Erase Board Used to Enhance Lecture

There are many uses for wall charts, and for this reason, I love utilizing them in my training sessions. I always include wall charts as a necessity in my Trainers Toolkit.

Training Videos

I love the use of videos in training. They add another element to the training that can be used to teach learners and are often used to emphasize key concepts and relate to real-life situations. They can be used to demonstrate tasks and can be helpful when facilitating almost any type of training. Some videos are an excellent way to give the participants a break from lectures and give the facilitator a short break as well. Videos in training also serve well as ice-breakers or to drive a point the facilitator is trying to make. I have found short humorous videos useful to provide a boost of energy after breaks or lunches. Videos can be used to inspire a call to action or to invoke some other specific emotion from the audience like empathy or excitement during Customer Service, Soft Skills or Sales training. They can be used as a bridge to connect learners to the subject matter.

Another way I have used videos is to play a recording of previous training. This works with online training, where I record the training and post it to the LMS system. This way, people who may not have been able to attend can go online and watch the recording. Also, anyone can go back and watch it if they missed anything or want to view it as a refresher. In other words, the video itself can be the training!

How many times have you wanted to fix something around the house or complete a task on your computer or smartphone but didn't know how? I bet chances are you went to YouTube and watched a video and learned how to do it! Just like that, ten minutes later,

"Videos can be used to inspire a call to action or to invoke some other specific emotion from the audience."

you've accomplished the task. It doesn't matter if it is learning how to use formulas in a Microsoft Excel spreadsheet to impress your manager or learning the latest dance moves you saw your nieces and nephews doing so you can impress them at the next family function. That is the power of video training.

In Technical Training, we often use videos to show the participants how to perform an action in the system. Considering learners over the years have developed shorter attention spans, many people have even started to create Micro-Videos. These are videos that are one to two minutes in length. You can use them to share an idea or a short process and can be easily accessible to the learners. Since you cannot print out a video, be sure to include the links to the video or send them to the participant after the training.

Props

Props *can be used to involve the class by keeping them interested, engaged, and, most of all, awake*! You can use props that are related to the subject matter or use them as a learning tool. I once had a professor that was into football. Because the instructor loved football, he brought one to the class and tossed it to people when he wanted them to answer a question. It was great because you never knew who he would throw the football to, which caused you to pay attention in the class, and this kept us on

"Props can be used to involve the class by keeping them interested, engaged, and most of all awake!"

our toes. I have witnessed speakers use various props during training. For example, baseball bats, basketballs, lunchboxes, old outdated computers, backpacks, brooms, multiple versions of cell phones, board games, and all types of items as props to emphasize specific points they wanted to make.

For Auditory Learners Use Lectures, Sound Bites and Speaking Opportunities

Auditory learners learn by listening, so they tend to learn well with lectures. You can give them verbal instructions, and they will be able to recite the steps when the person next to them asks, "What did the instructor say to do?" When I trained Contact Center agents at a health care company, I had a couple of exercises where the trainees had to listen to different types of calls they would encounter once they completed training. Since learning activities work well for auditory learners, I created an exercise where people would have to use their listening skills. Below are two examples of how I used phone calls to enhance Contact Center training in the Healthcare industry.

Example One: Pre-Recorded Calls

To enhance the learning in a training session, I facilitated an exercise using pre-recorded calls. I instructed the trainees a caller was calling into the appointment center to make an appointment, and they were the Contact Center Agent answering the phone. Their job was to take the call and assist the caller with what they needed. I played the call for the class in its entirety and then asked a series of questions about the interaction:

- What was the name of the caller?
- What service were they calling about?
- Who needed the appointment or service?
- When did they need the service?
- Was there anything else the caller needed?

The agents listening skills were vital because they were responsible for documenting the following information in the electronic medical record:

- Name
- Date of Birth
- Event Type
- Call Details
- Provider Name
- Appointment Date/Time

When I asked the interaction questions, rarely did everyone answer correctly after the first time I played the call. This is the reason recorded calls worked so well in training; because I could pause, rewind, and replay the calls to point out and confirm what they heard correctly and what they missed. I asked those particular questions so the trainees could become comfortable with the conversations they were having. Yes, they are conversations and not interviews or just a list of questions. **PEOPLE ARE NOT ROBOTS!** Speaking to people is not just running through a checklist monotone and indifferent. I teach my trainees that you talk to your customers or patients similar to when you are having a casual **professional** conversation. Notice I said casual **professional** conversation. I stress the word professional because when I tell people to have a casual conversation, they sometimes tend to think they can completely tone it all the way down, and that is not what I am saying. You want to make people feel comfortable so that you can get the information you need but still be a professional and handle their needs in a business manner.

Example Two: Live Call Listening

For this exercise, I partnered with the Contact Center Leadership and invited a Subject Matter Expert to my training to take live calls for the class. This way, the trainees could see their jobs in action at full speed. They were not allowed to ask any questions until the call ended and had to use their listening skills. This would be their reality in a couple of weeks. It was important they experienced the job and were allowed the opportunity to ask questions before they were on their own. The class benefited from hearing an experienced agent take calls. They listened to which types of calls came in, which types of questions the callers had, and how the agent responded to those inquiries. After the call was completed, the trainees could ask as many questions as they wanted to get a better understanding of the job and were able to imagine themselves on the call.

Listening to calls is a style of training that also works well with some sales teams because new sales agents get to hear how experienced sales agents handle themselves on real sales calls. These are not theoretical principles and theories; no, these are actual calls with real customers in a protected environment. I have used this method of training in calibration sessions with quality and leadership teams, as well. Listening to what the employees are saying and how they are communicating with the customers can be a massive opportunity for organizations. This information can be used to flush out existing issues and improve processes and the quality of the training as well. In my experience, listening to calls (or call monitoring) can lead to changing antiquated methods. Training departments can be an integral part of the documentation and re-education process for organizations. Which is why it is important for them to be involved in the process early on. What can you do if you do not have access to recorded calls? You can recreate them. It will take some time and a couple of experienced people to record the calls, but it will be well worth it in the end. The benefit of doing this is you can create precisely the type of scenario and include all of the information you want. The calls will be heard exactly how you wrote them. If you cannot record phone calls through your system, some devices will even make it sound like you are on a real phone call. Just go on Google, and you can find them.

One last thing you can do for Auditory Learners is to play music at convenient times throughout the training. Music may not be directly connected to the learning but can help to set the mood in the room. Soft music played can relax the room while more upbeat music can excite the room and get them pumped up while performing a learning exercise. One thing to remember about music is to ensure the music is appropriate. Some music can contain offensive language, which can and will turn into an HR issue, so beware of the music you choose to play. Jazz music is a consistent choice for me because many songs do not have lyrics for anyone to take offense to. There are a variety of upbeat or slow tempo songs available. Holiday music is a great option as well during certain times of the year, as most people enjoy it, and it makes the class feel more festive during the holiday season.

For Kinesthetic Learners, Let Them Do It

Kinesthetic learners like to touch and feel things. In training, they need to be able to have hands-on practice. You can talk to them for hours, but until they get the opportunity to try it themselves, the information will not truly sink in. Kinesthetic learners want you to show them how to do something, and they want to be able to follow along while you are doing it. For these types of trainees, I like to give them something to do with their hands while I facilitate lectures or show lengthy videos. Sometimes I will offer fidget widgets or little toys to those who would otherwise disrupt the class while they listen to a lecture. They want to be able to "**Do it,**" so the widgets keep their attention while other types of learning styles are being presented. Kinesthetic learners can't wait until they get the chance to try the activity themselves, so the widgets act as a buffer in the meantime. I design my training courses to include hands-on exercises because I know Kinesthetic learners usually appreciate them. I believe it makes for a better learning experience. First, you must explain the instructions to the learners and then have the learners demonstrate their understanding of the exercise by performing the activity. You can have kinesthetic learners complete the activity while they are seated, or you can have them volunteer to come up to the facilitator's desk to complete the activity in front of the class. I have received the most positive feedback from learners participating in hands-on exercises, which is why I always include them in my classes.

CHAPTER 3
MAKE LEARNING FUN

Question: I facilitate Technical Training, which is pretty boring. How do I make my training fun?

Answer: Any training can be fun, especially when you engage the learners. Some of my favorite things to liven up technical training is to facilitate educational exercises or games to keep everyone involved and interested in the class.

This chapter contains information on the following topics:
- **Learning Activities**
- **Educational Games (Activities)**
- **Computer Simulated Activities**
- **The FISH! Philosophy**

"My philosophy is: If you can't have fun, there's no sense in doing it." – Paul Walker

Learning Activities

When I was a Training Specialist, I facilitated all types of different courses. I've done Soft Skills, Technical, Refresher, New Hire Orientation, Human Resources, and many other types of training. Out of all of them, I believe Technical Training has provided the most significant challenge. Let's face it, Technical Training does not always include the most exciting subject matter, but there are ways that you can make it fun. Some of the techniques include individual and group activities, learning games, scavenger hunts, and other types of exercises to keep the classroom interesting. All of these things are geared towards training retention and getting the participants to remember the information that they learned without putting them to sleep. This is the difference between average trainers and successful facilitators. The ordinary trainer's goal is strictly to get through the material by the end of the class. Successful facilitators get involved, and make sure their participants learned everything they need to know. They also captivate the audience while doing so. Successful facilitators teach in a way that keeps you interested and wanting to learn more. Great ones do it so well that sometimes you don't even know that you're learning. That's the whole point, great facilitators make learning fun, engaging, and have the participants walk away loaded with the knowledge they need to do their jobs. Great facilitators also involve the learners in the action and provide the much-needed tools to encourage the learning process.

"Any type of training can be made fun especially when you engage the learners."

Whatever the trainees need, they should get, and they deserve to receive an excellent training experience. I also tell people that part of the training experience comes from the energy in the classroom. Early in my career, when I facilitated training classes, I would get a large amount of energy from the participants. I had to feel a certain vibe to get fully into it. If the class had low energy, I was tired and sluggish. If they had high energy, then I would bounce off the walls. My energy level mirrored the room. Later as I became a more seasoned facilitator, I learned the opposite to be true. The participants fed off my energy. I realized it was up to me to set the tone in the room, but I still communicated with the audience they had an active responsibility in the liveliness of the classroom. This also gave me their buy-in, and with their buy-in, I was halfway there. Then all I had to do was deliver great content! Remember, it is up to you to make the experience fun and exciting for the learners.

Educational Games (Activities)

One way to make training fun is to include educational games. Over the years, educational games, or learning activities, (You don't want to call it a game because people will think you are not working or being productive) have become increasingly popular in classrooms and training rooms. Popular game shows can all be modified for educational use, and the participants love them, especially if there are prizes involved!

- Jeopardy
- $100,000 Pyramid

- Cash Cab
- Family Feud
- How to Be a Millionaire
- Charades

The good thing about using educational games (learning activities) is it encourages healthy competition, retention of the information, and are just plain fun. They can be used with both young and adult learners and are easy to facilitate. You can create your own or purchase out of the box versions that can be adapted you your industry from various sources online. Using educational games (or activates) engages the learners in a way that using only lectures does not.

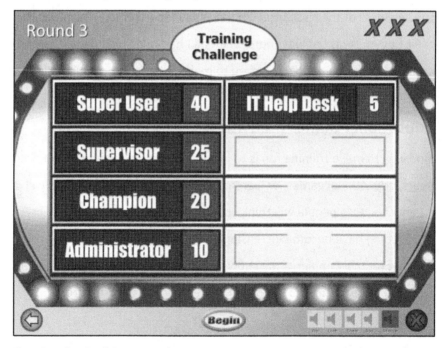

Figure 3.1 Educational Game Example

Computer Simulated Activities

Another way to make learning fun is to use computer-simulated activities. In my experience, using games to prepare for a test or quiz provides increased positive results. The game or activity should be fun and remove some of the stress and risk from performing a procedure, "practicing" on actual live patients, or using live data to run simulations. A simulation of the techniques involved in a complicated surgery is an excellent example of how to use a computer-simulated activity. These types of learning activities have become popular in industries that include STEAM (Science, Technology, Engineering, Arts, and Mathematics) related concepts. Computer simulations have become a mainstay in many classrooms and workplaces and have various benefits, including industries like:

- Healthcare
- Information Technology
- Automotive/Aerospace
- Manufacturing/Construction
- Media and Film
- Finance

All these industries require some training and education, and all of these can be taught or reinforced in part by using an educational learning format. Think about it, a surgeon, architect, and math teacher all start as students and require training and education. Here are some examples of how learning can be taught or reinforced by using educational games or activities in those professions:

- A medical student performs a complicated procedure on a computerized simulated program before operating on a live person
- An engineering student builds a computerized draft model of a new design for a skyscraper before building it
- A mathematics teacher creates a learning game for other students to solve mathematical equations in the classroom

These are just a few examples. I have listed a few more industries and professions in the illustration below and how they relate to STEAM careers. Again, all of these industries require learning and education, so there will be opportunities to use a learning game or simulation during training.

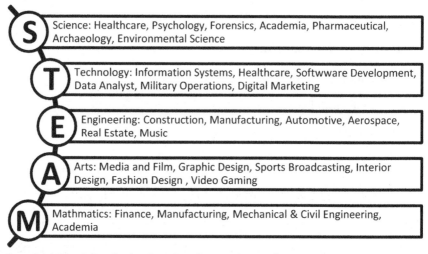

Figure 3.1 STEAM-Related Industries Using Educational Games/Activities

What other examples of learning games or simulations could you perform while training in your industry?

The Fish Philosophy

People would often ask me why I am always so happy at work. I would tell them, "The day I stop having fun at work is the day I start looking for a new job." That still rings true today. Paul Walker's quote, *"My philosophy is: If you can't have fun, there's no sense in doing it."* resonates with me because I too believe if you are not having fun, what is the point? That's not to say that I never have a bad day. I have challenging days, high-pressure situations, and stressful projects, just like anyone else. However, when every day starts to take more enjoyment than what it gives, I begin to question what and why I am doing what it is I'm doing. It may sound cliché, but life is very short, and I will not repeatedly spend my time somewhere that makes me unhappy. Most of my adult life I have lived by this principle. It took me a while to understand it, but once I got it, I have been locked in ever since. I am not saying the minute something makes me unhappy I quit my job. (Over the last 16 years I have only worked for three companies.) What I am saying is that when things start to make me unhappy at work, I begin the process of re-evaluating the reasons I keep showing up. If there is no longer love or desire, or the stress outweighs the contribution, then I start looking for a new place to take my passion and talent where I can have fun too!

"The day I stop having fun at work is the day I start looking for a new job."

When it comes to having fun at work, I took a page from the playbook created by the guys at the Pike Place Fish Market in Seattle, Washington. The gentlemen at the world-famous fish market were the inspiration for a book and video called **FISH! A Proven Way to Boost Morale and Improve Results** written by Stephen C. Lundin, Ph.D., Harry Paul, and John Christensen. I learned about FISH! and Pike Place Fish Market while working in a Contact Center at UnitedHealth Group. It was a part of our customer service training at the time and enhanced the way I viewed my work. There were powerful lessons in the training which have stuck with me for almost two decades.

John Yokoyama was an employee working at an ordinary fish market. His boss was tired of running the business and approached John about taking over the market. This was not the first time John's boss had asked him to take over the market. John had turned his boss down before; however, John's circumstances had changed. He was finally ready and agreed to take over the fish market. John did not know how to lead his staff, did not have a good feeling about how the market was performing, was frustrated with the morale and the way he was leading his workers. John decided it was time for a change and hired a business consultant to work with them on improving the team. A life-changing event for John, his workers, and the market came next.

To get all of the details, I suggest you purchase a copy of the book or the video. You can find clips of the video on YouTube, but I will discuss one of the main principles that helped me define my perspective on work and training.

The guys at the fish market took a tedious job and figured out a way to have fun with it. They literally started throwing fish from one side of the market to the other and incidentally started to put on a show during their workday. The fish guys began to have fun, and the customers started to have fun with them, which increased the sales and notoriety of the market. Miraculously, the attitudes of doing what was sometimes back-breaking work improved dramatically. As a bonus, because of their new-found freedom, fun, and fulfilling work-attitudes, Pike Place Fish Market became World Famous! One of the gentlemen in the video said, "There is always a choice about the way you do your work, even if there is not a choice about the work itself." When I heard that statement, I was hooked! I thought, Wow! If they can do that with their jobs, then I can make my job enjoyable and have fun every day, which is what I did. I started to enjoy my training classes and interactions with co-workers even more! It became infectious. Pretty soon many of the trainers around me were having fun and talking about enjoying their classes more as well. People started to comment on what was happening and asked what my "secret" to being so happy at work all of the time was. Supervisors started sending the other trainers to shadow me in my classes to see what I was doing! It was a humbling experience and a great time in my life and career.

I know each company is different; we all can't throw fish around our offices to have fun at work. I started hosting workshops and asking people what they could do in their workplace to make things fun? "What are some ways you can Play at work?" This began to make people think differently about the way they went about their day, and for a while, I saw a positive shift in morale in the training department. I would like to believe it also improved in other departments as well.

I will end this chapter with a quote that struck a chord with me from John Yokoyama, owner of the Pike Place Fish Market. If the workers at the fish market can have this type of attitude towards their work, imagine what kind of impact it could have on you and yours.

"At the World Famous Pike Place Fish Market, we know that it's possible for each of us as human beings to impact the way other people experience life. Through our work, we're out to improve the quality of life for everyone. We are working inside the possibility of world peace and prosperity for all people. This is our commitment -that's who we are - it's what we do." – John Yokoyama

CHAPTER 4
SOFT SKILLS

Question: What are soft skills, and why do I need them in training?

Answer: If you don't know what soft skills are, then you are already in trouble. Soft skills are customer service. They are those skills your mother should have taught you at home. Being polite, using please and thank you, calling people by their names, and recognizing and helping people when they need it are all examples of soft skills. You need them because they are fundamental human decencies and will get you further than being rude to people will.

This chapter contains information on the following topics:
- Soft Skills
- Customer Service
- Connecting with the Class
- Relating to the Learners
- Using Real Life Stories

"You cannot continuously improve interdependency systems and processes until you progressively perfect interdependent, interpersonal relationships." – Stephen Covey

Soft Skills

Emotional Intelligence, Story-Telling, and other soft-skills are invaluable techniques in learning and training. Using your Soft Skills or Emotional Intelligence can gain you much needed emotional currency that can be spent relating to and winning over your participants. You may ask, "What does customer service have to do with training? I am great with my customers and am just conducting training for internal staff." Or, "Why are we talking about customer service in a technical training class?" It is surprising to me when people have these types of questions, and I get it more often than I would like to. People just don't think it's that important which baffles me.

When I consult with organizations on how to improve their customer service, the first thing I do is observe. I see employees pass each other in the hallways without speaking, being rude in person and over email, and not living the company's mission, vision, or values. For example, if you say, *Employees are our greatest assets.*, but tell your employees they are expendable, I'd say you are not living the mission. I would point out it is **not** your mission, and **you** surely don't value your staff! Those words are just some words you see on the wall in your corporate lobby or sound cute in a new hire packet or advertisement. What many leaders and trainers fail to realize is by not implementing and training customer service and how it relates to the employees at all levels (no matter what the job is) is training their staff on how to interact with each other and their customers as well. If you think, no, as long as we treat the customer well, it doesn't matter how we treat each other, you better think again. That's like when your parents gave you the "Do as I say and not as I do" speech. It didn't work then, and it won't work now. People learn by example, and leadership must lead by example. Great leadership makes happy employees; and, happy employees make satisfied customers. For all of my trainers out there, just in case you hadn't realized it, **Training** is a part of **Leadership**. In essence **you** are a part of leadership. This is why I cover soft skills and customer service when conducting T3 sessions and in my end user training classes.

Customer Service

Whatever happened to customer service? Common courtesies like please and thank you, and yes sir, no ma'am go a long way. In my opinion, customer service as a whole is dead, at least the way I knew it when I started my career. Common sense and common courtesy seem a thing of the past, and people don't care the same way they used to. Workers must be told when to be polite, when to ask if customers need anything else, or how else they could help the customer. It's a shame, but times have changed quite a bit, and we have to adapt. (Or do we?)

One morning I was on my way to work and felt my stomach growl. I didn't get a chance to eat breakfast before I hit the road because I was running late but was pretty hungry. I was able to make up some time on the freeway, and as a result, I stopped at Chick-Fil-A to grab a quick bite to eat. I pulled into the drive-thru and was greeted by the voice in the speaker box. I spoke into the box to order

"For all of my trainers out there, just in case you hadn't realized it, Training is a part of Leadership.."

my food. The voice in the speaker repeated my order. I thanked the person who took my order. I am always polite to the people in the foodservice industry.

> *1. Because it is the right thing to do.*

> *2. Because I don't want anyone to do anything to my food that I may regret later.*

What happened next was almost magical. The voice in the box said, "My pleasure." Huh? "What was that?" I asked. The voice in the box said, "I said it is my pleasure." Wow! Instantly my mind was blown. The worker expressed to me it was her pleasure to take my order at 6:30 in the morning. This was amazing! As I pulled around the corner, I handed the young lady my debit card to pay for my meal. She swiped the card, gave it back, and I smiled as I pulled up to the second window. The gentleman gave me my food, and I asked for some strawberry jam. He threw a couple of packets of jam in my bag, and after I said, "Thank you." The young man replied, "My pleasure." I drove off thinking, man! Those two were fantastic at providing customer service; they really get it. They made it their pleasure to serve and do it with a smile.

On another morning, I went through the drive-through at a different fast-food restaurant and had a completely different experience. I placed my order, the attendant repeated my order, I thanked them, and when I did, the person told me to pull around to the first window. Whoa! Where was the warm and fuzzy, "My pleasure?" Was this person not pleased to take my order this early in the morning? I pulled to the first window, paid for my food, pulled forward to the second window, and was given my food. That was it. I drove off feeling unvalued as a customer. It was not their pleasure, and they could have cared less if I patronized their business or not. I was just order #1227. Now, this may not have been the intent, but it sure felt like it. I felt those people just did not care at all.

The next time I went through the drive-thru at Chick-Fil-A, I received my warm and fuzzy, "My pleasure and Thank you." After a few more visits, I started sharing my experience with other people in the service industry. I found out it was part of their script, and I thought it was pure genius. (Someone in the Chick-Fil-A organization must have had some home training,) Implementing the simple practice of saying, "Please, Thank You, and My Pleasure" made me feel welcomed and appreciated. I still smile when I hear it. That's terrific Customer Service!

Connect with the Class

I picked up many skills while facilitating training classes. One of the things I learned was that you could quickly gain credibility by using simple techniques. Calling people by their names is one of those techniques. I used to travel frequently as a Training Specialist and would occasional co-facilitate classes with other trainers. One of the sessions I co-facilitated was four-weeks in length. Each trainer facilitated the class for two weeks, so we were never in the classroom at the same time. During this particular training I was responsible for facilitating the second half of the class. I introduced myself to the trainees and conducted a simple Tent-Card Ice-Breaker activity. Tent cards are a great way to help you remember participants' names and get to know a little about them. The ice-breaker had them create a tent card that displayed their name and an illustration of what makes them happy, like a person, hobby, or pet. As I interacted with the class, I addressed the individuals by name and asked them how the class was going. As we talked, one gentleman named Adam stopped me and said, "Excuse me. I just want to say that I appreciate the way you call us by our names." He must have read the confused look on my face. He laughed and said, "You know, the last trainer was here for two weeks and never called us by our names, hardly made eye contact with us, and it really makes a difference." I apologized for the experience they had and assured Adam that I would be engaging him and the entire class. I told them this would be an interactive class, we would all engage each other, and we would all get to know one other over the next two weeks. This was perhaps one of the best experiences in a class that summer and the most impactful for both the trainees and me. A gesture as simple as calling people by their name can mean so much to a person and proved to be the turning point in this class. They were now focused, attentive and in tune with the learning. This was one of the most fun and memorable training classes I had ever facilitated.

Relate to the Learners

People learn better when they can relate to you and what you are saying. Therefore, you must learn to connect with people. If you have started your class off correctly, you will have conducted an ice-breaker that will give you information about the people in your training session. The purpose of the ice-breakers is not just to go through the motions of a training exercise. During these activities, you should be gathering valuable information or data about your participants. You will learn:

"A gesture as simple as calling people by their name can mean so much to a person and proved to be the turning point in this class."

- Who is an animal lover and attends dog shows?
- Who is athletic and likes to hike or run marathons?
- Who is into racecars and attends local drag races?
- Who likes baking and watches the food network?
- Who likes to go to swap meets and collect antiques?
- Who has school-aged kids into sports or theater activities?
- Who is into real estate and watches HGTV on the weekends?
- Who is an avid reader and can swap book recommendations?

All these things are high-quality emotional intelligence clues that can help you relate to the people in your classes. The important thing is for you not to patronize people. You have to actually care about the topic you are discussing. The feeling must be genuine because people can see and feel it if it is not real. If you fake it, you run the risk of offending your learners and losing the connection.

Use Real Life Stories

How do you gain credibility, illicit buy-in, and create long-lasting bonds with those you interact with? You are often able to accomplish this by sharing real stories from your life and your experiences. To reiterate, using real-life examples is a way to accelerate learning. People connect to you when they can see themselves in you. When they hear a story about how you used the concepts and principles you are teaching them successfully, then this speeds up the learning process. Don't believe me? Google **The Power of Story-Telling** and read through some of the results. There have been articles, blog posts, and books written about the power story-telling has and how others have leveraged this strategy to their advantage to create success in their business and their personal lives. When I conduct training classes, I make a habit of using my own life experiences, case studies and on the job instances as methods of facilitation. This helps me connect with the trainees I'm teaching, especially when it's in an industry in which I have a lot of experience. In healthcare, I am particularly successful in using case studies in Provider Training because that is how they learn in school and during residency. Learning never stops, and there are many variations of conditions that require preparation. People frequently want to know that you have been in their position, and it's always good to connect with the people who have been where they are going. It also makes it fun in the classroom when the stories are a bit humorous. Trainees also want to know that they are not alone and will make it through the situations and tasks at hand. If you can tell someone, "Hey, if I can make it, you can make it," that eases some of the anxiety they may be feeling.

CHAPTER 5
CLASS MANAGEMENT

Question: How can I help everyone and take care of administrative tasks, like recording attendance, the same day if I'm training the class?
Answer: Class management is vital to success, and one of those skills that often gets forgotten. People don't really think about class management until something goes wrong.

This chapter contains information on the following topics:
- **Time and Attendance**
- **Work the Room**
- **Utilize your spare time**

Learning is not attained by chance, it must be sought for with ardor and attended with diligence." – Abigail Adams

Time and Attendance

At some point, someone in leadership will want to know what is going on in the training department. You will also want to know what the ROI or Return on Investment from all the fantastic training you have been delivering. In this book, I won't go into details of the many data points you could report on, but at a bare minimum, you should be recording time and attendance. In other words, you should be able to track and verify who you have trained and if they attended the entire session. Most likely, management will want to know about the attendance from a payroll perspective as well. (If the trainee did not attend the training you don't want to have to pay them.) Tracking attendance can be accomplished in a couple of ways. You can track it digitally or analog. If you have a system that supports badging in and out with a key card or badge, you can track attendance that way. The record keeping system should be able to allow you to produce all of the necessary detail regarding attendance. If not, you can go old school and have people sign a Sign-In-Sheet that has their name, ID Number, and the department where they work. Having someone's signed signature does have its advantages. There will be a time when you will have to show proof that someone attended a training (or did not attend the session), and having their signature is as good as it gets. Either way, you want the information to feed into your Learning Management System (LMS) for recordkeeping. If the badging system can electronically transmit the data to your LMS, that would be optimal; if not, the trainer will have to enter the attendance records manually. Having those records allows you to report things like: How many attendees you had month over month or whether the participants are completing all days of a multi-day training course. This information can help you track and trend the data to determine things like:

- Do we have enough training staff?
- Are the dates and times of training correct for the organization?
- Are we offering too many or not enough classes?

These are all valuable data points in the world of training and education.

Work the Room

Facilitation and class management has come a long way. Being in a classroom where the facilitator is standing in the front of the classroom behind the podium and talking for an hour straight is tough. Many people do not learn well this way. To increase the success of your class, you must be engaging. Part of the way you do this is to work your room. This means coming out from behind the podium, lectern, or facilitator's desk and interact with your group. When you are conducting technical training, how do you know if the participants in the class are on the same page or screen as you? You have to walk around the room, check to see what's going on, and help people who get stuck. If you stand in front of the classroom and ask a question like, "Are you all with me?" people will say yes and nod their heads yes, even if they are not with you! It's the craziest thing. People would rather be lost and try to figure it out before you realize it, than raise their hand and say, "I need help." As a facilitator, it is your responsibility to observe and understand what is going on in the room. You should know who is advanced and who is struggling. There are simple adjustments and systems you can put in place to identify these things to help the participants feel at ease. Once you have

"As a facilitator it is your responsibility to observe and understand what is going on in the room."

assessed the situation, if you notice someone is a slower learner, pair them up with someone who catches on quickly. If someone can't see from the back of the room. Switch the seating arrangements on a break or lunch. But you won't know any of this unless you are up, being observant, attentive, communicating, and working your room. Average trainers will stand behind a podium the entire class or sit at their desk and wait for people to ask them a question. Successful trainers who work the room do not wait for people to come to them, they go to the learners. They incite meaningful discussions, involve the classroom in group discussions, help people individually and can tell when a break is needed because they know what is going on and are in tune with their classrooms.

Utilize your Spare Time

Utilizing your spare time is crucial when managing a training class, especially if you are the only trainer in the class. Yes, sometimes you may have the luxury of having another trainer or training assistant in your session. Reasons for this could be:

- There are be a large number of attendees (Over 20 or 30 participants depending on the type of training)
- You are mentoring/training someone to become a trainer (T3)

- You have a Subject Matter Expert or Super User assisting in your training

All those scenarios may require assistance in the classroom, but what if you do not have access to any of those resources, and you are on your own? Like many of us, you will have to manage your time wisely. You may even have to get creative at times. I have had this conversation with trainers many times throughout my career as a Training Manager, mentor, and consultant. Trainers will tell me, "I don't have time to log attendance, or score quizzes or check my email," or whatever the task is they are trying to avoid at the moment. To this, I would ask them, "What were you doing while the class was watching the 15-minute video on customer service?" When they reply, they were watching it with them; I ask how many times they had seen the video? They'd tell me they have seen it more than a few times; so I'd ask, "Why are **you** still watching the video?" The trainer could probably facilitate that portion of the class without the actual video if they had to. Now, there is something to be said for room observation and watching your room for facial expressions, laughter, or people going to sleep during the course. This does add value; however, I can't tell you how many times I watched a set of customer service videos when I was a trainer at the beginning of my career. My fellow trainers and I would laugh as we quoted lines, word for word, from the videos that we thought were funny or memorable. After a while, we could probably re-enact the entire video if we wanted. I knew which parts the class would laugh at, which sections were more thought-provoking and which parts of the video people would have comments and questions. Pretty soon, I figured out rather than continue to re-watch these videos over and over; I could use this time more efficiently by doing something else while the trainees were watching the videos. Remember those pesky attendance recording task trainers must do? Yup, you guessed it. I would press play on a video and complete attendance. This also works well while the trainees are finishing a self-led activity, like preparing for a teach-back. During this time, I would read my notes for the next lecture or exercise or complete another administrative task.

Encourage Class Participation

I am not sure I should give you these next tips because I feel like I'm giving away my best stuff here, but since you invested the time to read through this book, I will share it with you. (And again, I love to teach!) We all know audience or class participation is critical to the success of any training session, and it is sometimes difficult to get the participants to get involved. There are a few ways I have learned to master the art of class participation. First, you must have an infectious presentation style that invites people to participate. By this I mean, because of your energy and flow, people will want to get involved and have fun or engage in a lively discussion. If your skills are not there yet as a speaker or presenter, don't worry, you can learn to become a more engaging facilitator. In the meanwhile, I have detailed some of the techniques you can use to guarantee classroom participation. These tools are easy to implement and will help you to become a successful facilitator.

Use Incentives, Give-Aways, and Prizes

Incentives or giveaways are a great way to get people involved and excited about participating. Believe it or not, good old candy will frequently do the trick when trying to get people to volunteer in a classroom. Next time you are having trouble getting volunteers, ask a question, and when someone participates or gives the correct answer, give them a piece of candy and watch what happens. You'd be surprised what a small piece of candy will do to encourage someone to participate in the conversation. This does not make my facilitators in Dental Training happy, but it was a great way to get people to answer questions, even if they had to sacrifice their teeth a little. (Besides, they can always brush after.)

In most workplaces, stress can be a significant factor. Learning how to deal with stress, reducing stress or avoiding stress is a fact of life and comes with the territory. I use other people's stress to my advantage, and in my sessions, I learned to distribute a valuable commodity as a prize, stress balls. You know those palm-sized balls that you can grab and squeeze to relieve stress instead of grabbing another person when stressed? Those seem to be a big hit with the classes I facilitate. They come in all shapes, colors, sizes, and even come in fun customized shapes like footballs, baseballs, basketballs, and soccer balls as well. They can be used as great marketing tools as well by getting your company or department name, logo and contact information printed on them.

"Believe it or not, a good old piece of candy oftentimes will do the trick when trying to get people to volunteer in a classroom."

Items like these can be purchased online at a reasonable cost and are great to get the class interested in joining in the fun. Below is a list of giveaways or incentives I use in my training sessions:

- Candy
- Stress Balls
- Ink Pens
- Highlighters
- Fidget Widgets
- Notebooks
- T-Shirts
- Polo Shirts
- Sweat Shirts
- Coffee Mugs/Water Bottles/Cups
- Cell Phone Chargers

Have a Ringer in the Audience!

Many times, getting that first person to participate in a training session is one of the toughest things to do. Once that first-person opens themselves up, it allows others to feel comfortable in asking their question(s) as well. Knowing someone is going to break the participation ice, not to mention having it be a controlled question, makes it that much easier to facilitate the class. Having assurance that someone will participate and ask questions is like having an ace in my back pocket. This way, I know for sure someone will engage, and when they do, others will join in as well. So How do I guarantee that things will go my way and that someone will respond to me when I ask for audience participation? I use what I call a "Ringer." What is a ringer? Someone who I have designated in advance to ask questions during the beginning of class. I love to do this with especially difficult crowds. If I know in advance that I will have opposition to class participation, I will pull someone aside before the session starts and ask them if they would be willing to participate. I usually sweeten the deal by giving them a prize. I will provide them with a question or set of questions to ask ahead of time and instruct them when to ask the questions. Then I use that question or questions to spark conversation during the training. Another thing you can do is use yourself as the ringer. Instead of selecting someone to ask prepared targeted questions directly, use yourself as the ringer by indirectly adding yourself in the mix. One way to do this is to have your participants write down questions they have about the training onto 3x5 index cards, which you will answer later during the training. Then you add a couple of your own question cards to the stack of questions the audience asked to ensure you get specific inquiries from the group. This works well because the questions are "anonymous." You get to answer questions given by the audience members and those specifically targeted to the topic chosen by you as well. This technique works best when you have larger audiences. When used with classes with fewer participants, people may discover they did not ask the questions you included, which could ruin your

"Instead of selecting someone to directly ask prepared targeted questions, use yourself as the ringer by including yourself in the mix."

credibility. A different way to include those essential items and retain your credibility is to advise the class that you have added some questions and answers that have been helpful to other training classes.

CHAPTER 6
FACILITATION TECHNIQUES AND MORE

Question: What other teaching techniques are out there? I thought you just stand in front of the class and talk.

Answer: Absolutely not! Just like there are different learning styles, there are so many different facilitation techniques.

This chapter contains information on the following topics:

- **Facilitation Styles**
    - Lectures
    - Breakout Sessions
    - Question and Answer or Q&A
    - Training Videos
    - Teach-Backs
    - Toss-Back Method
    - Live Example Training
    - OJT or On the Job Training
- **Periodically Check/Test for Understanding and Retention**
- **Show Em, Don't tell Em!**
- **Do Not Give Them Everything, Teach Them to Fish**
- **Do They Know Where to Find It?**

"Tell me and I forget, teach me and I may remember, involve me and I learn." – Benjamin Franklin

Facilitation Styles

Training is all about facilitation, so I'm going to take a little time here. Different environments call for different training methods. Using various training techniques to facilitate learning in classes benefits not only the participants but the trainer as well.

Mixing it up keeps people engaged, caters to the different learning styles, and (in some cases) keeps everyone from falling asleep! Some of the facilitation methods I use are as follows:

- Lectures
- Breakout Sessions
- Question and Answer or Q&A
- Training Videos
- Teach-Backs
- Toss-Back Method
- Live Example Training
- OJT or On the Job Training

Lectures

In-person lecturing is probably the most commonly used method of training but is certainly not the only way to teach a class. Lectures usually appeal most to auditory learners. The trainer stands in front of the classroom and conveys the information by speaking. Sometimes, the speaker uses a whiteboard or easel chart to pair with the lecture as a visual aid. For the most part, the main focal point is the trainer or teacher speaking to the participants. Many people think of lectures as old fashioned, long, and boring, but there are some fascinating and exciting lectures

"Using various training techniques to facilitate learning in classes benefits not only the participants but the trainer as well."

out there. T.E.D. Talks provide masterful examples of persuasive speeches. You can easily find these on YouTube. The most effective T.E.D. Talk videos I have seen have speakers who are dynamic, somewhat funny and know how to keep you on the edge of your seat waiting on the next sentence or the next word. If you want to be a great presenter, invest some time watching TED Talks and make sure you practice your material.

Another thing you can do is join your local chapter of Toastmasters. Toastmasters is a non-profit organization dedicated to helping people who want to become better public speakers. I have been a member of Toastmasters and highly recommend it to new and experienced trainers. I required my team of trainers to attend Toastmasters for a time to improve their skills and see how other people in other settings spoke to audiences. There are also videos on YouTube of past and present speech contest champions that will change the way you think about speaking and training when giving lectures.

Breakout Sessions

Breakout sessions work well when you have at least four or more participants in a class. Breaking up the group into smaller groups of two or more to review what was just taught or come up with ideas on how they can use the information just learned is a great way to get people moving around, brainstorming, and communicating with each other. The facilitator should monitor the conversations, add input where necessary, and answer any questions the groups may have. Breakout sessions should be used in short bursts (5 - 20 minutes) and could be related to the content or unrelated if being used as an ice-breaker.

Question and Answer or Q&A Sessions

During training, you want to check for understanding of the content or material presented. A simple way to verify the participants understand what you are teaching is to ask them questions:

- What was one thing you learned from the section we just covered?
- What stood out the most from the material today?
- What were the key concepts from the lecture?
- What is one concept you can apply to your work tomorrow?

Questions can be a great way to check for understanding, test out whether your audience is paying attention or not, and see what type of crowd you are dealing with. Questions can be tricky if you don't know the audience, so during class, you should pay attention to the climate of the classroom before asking certain people a question. You must know which participants are in the class to learn and which are there because they were **"Volun-told"** to be there. Making sure your audience is receptive to questions is critical. (You don't want to fuel the fire of people whose goal is to derail your class.) While most of the time, your participants will be responsive, keep an eye out for those who are not. You may not want to ask them questions unless you are being strategic and asking those participants for a specific reason, like getting them involved in the class.

Training Videos

I like using Training Videos in my courses because they can be an excellent way to break up the monotony of the lecture in the class or used just to switch things up. Depending on your industry, videos may be a necessary tool to facilitate learning. If you are in the automotive industry, it is acceptable to facilitate a lecture about how an internal combustion engine works. It would be even better to have CAD drawings illustration the various parts and pieces required to make the engine run. But watching a video on how the engine is put together by a team of people and then watching the engine start and run in a car is even better. In the healthcare industry, talking about how a heart transplant is performed may sound exciting to a medical student. They would probably enjoy it more if they saw pictures of the surgery. Watching a video of the operation occurring would provide more context and be more exciting! Videos can be cost-effective as well. After you make the initial purchase; then you will be able to reuse them over and over again.

Teach-Backs

Teach-backs are one of my absolute favorite learning activities. I have a theory that says, if you can teach what you have just learned, then most likely, you really understand it.

This method works well with groups and in one-on-one training sessions. In one-on-one trainings, you can teach the learner a concept, principle, or action and ask them to demonstrate what they have just learned. If the trainee can show you how to perform the requested action or complete a particular exercise on their own, they've got it. If they are not able to demonstrate what they have just learned, it is okay. This means the learner needs more training or review.

In group settings, I like to match people up in groups of two or more. I give each group a set amount of time to review a concept or section of the training. After the time is up, they must present to the rest of the class and teach the other learners the material for their part or topic of the training. I allow them to use whatever style of presentation they would like to use, visual, audio, or kinesthetic. In technical training, I strongly encourage or require them to use the system to facilitate the teach-back session since the systems are what they are there to learn. The participants are usually engaged, enjoy the teach-backs and get more from the course since they were involved in training a portion of the class. This satisfies a part of the Adult Learning Principles because adults like to learn by doing.

"If you can teach what you have just learned then most likely you really understand it."

The Toss-Back Method

The toss-back method of answering questions can be beneficial. It can be used to elicit audience participation when you want to poll the class or even when you do not know the answer to the question. Now I know what you are thinking. If you are the trainer, you should know anything and everything there is to know about the subject matter. Well, that is not the case all of the time. There will even be times when the participants in the class know more about the subject matter than you! The toss-back method is straightforward. When someone in your class asks a question, you ask it right back to the class. For example, someone asks, "How do I know if the trainees in my class are retaining the information?" Address the class and either repeat the question verbatim or ask, "What do you think the answer to this question is?" or "What are some possible answers to this question?" This works great if the question is a subjective one or when there are multiple answers to the question. You can use this to your advantage when you have an unusually quiet class, or you want to get the class engaged in the lesson. But what if you genuinely do not know the answer to the question? Tell them you do not know the answer but will research it and get back to them. It's just that simple. There are two keys to this method, though, to make it successful.

1. **Make sure to follow up with the person who asked the question or the entire class.**

One thing I do to accomplish this is I create a parking lot on a wall chart for questions that I cannot immediately answer. I will either have the participants write the question down on a sticky note, or do it myself, and stick the note on the chart. I let them know I will get back to them with the answer within a certain amount of time. The next break, lunch, or following day will work, but make sure you get back to them with the answer. Not following up can be one of the quickest ways to lose credibility with the person who had the question or the entire group.

2. **Do not overuse the Toss-Back Method**

The second factor in making the toss-back method successful is you must not overuse it. If you are tossing every question back to the audience, they will either know or think that you do not know anything. In the participants' eyes, it is the same, and will quickly ruin your credibility. The participants will tune out or stop asking questions, and that will hinder the learning process.

Live Training Examples

When I facilitated New Hire Training for Contact Center agents, I loved scheduling a Subject Matter Expert (SME) to come to my class and take live calls. I also had trainees sit side by side to shadow with an experienced agent so they could experience what their new job would be like in real-time. The trainees got to learn by hearing calls live and got to learn by watching how an experienced agent handled themselves currently. After the call was over, the trainees were allowed to pick the SME's brain and ask as many questions as they wanted. This served multiple purposes:

1. Learners got to see and hear a Subject Matter Expert in action
2. It gave me a bit of a break in the class
3. It allowed me to listen to some recent calls and validate my curriculum and the information I was teaching in the class was still current and up to date

Another way I used training examples was by playing recorded calls. The calls were not really "live" or taken in real-time, but they were real calls. Using these calls allowed me to stop, pause or replay the call as needed, let participants ask questions or people to replay something that they didn't hear. I started by playing the call in its entirety and asking the participants what they heard. Then I would restart the call, play portions of the call and pause it. I'd ask the participants what they heard, if they had enough information to proceed or if they needed me to replay the call to get more information. It worked great and using these calls was an awesome learning tool during the training. The calls gave them a real-life taste of what they would be dealing with on the job without the pressure of having someone on the line just yet. Doing this also allowed me to gauge the customer service skills of my trainees. I would ask them questions like "How do you think the agent handled the calls in terms of customer service? Was the agent polite, did they ask the caller if they could put them on hold? How long did they leave the customer on hold before returning to the call?" Because I also worked with the Call Quality Department, I would sometimes give the participants a Quality Call Scorecard and have them score the agents' calls. You'd be surprised how many trainees scored the calls tougher than I would have. It allowed me to teach them how the calls were scored and gave me leverage against them when it came time to score their calls. I'd say, "Remember how tough you scored that last call? Well, make sure that you take that into account when you are speaking with our customers." This helps them to put things into perspective and remember how important it is to conduct themselves when taking customer calls. If they would expect a certain level of service then they should certainly perform at that same level or higher as well.

OJT or On the Job Training

One of the funniest things to me is when a hiring manager thinks that after a few days of new hire training the employee is going to be "fully" trained and will be able to perform their job with the same level of proficiency as someone who has been on the job for years, hilarious right? Well, the managers don't think it is funny, and it is your job (or your leaders' job) to let the hiring manager know they have a responsibility after the classroom, called On the Job Training.

> *"New hire training classes are like Boot Camp to the military. You get basic skills and knowledge on how to conduct yourself, then you go off to war!"*

This may be facilitated by you as the trainer, if you are at a small organization or if the new hire stays with you until they are fully functioning. It depends on how your training structure is setup. For those who strictly conduct new hire training classes only, you will have to pass the baton after the class and help everyone understand, the training doesn't stop there. Much of the learning happens on the job. It could be working side-by-side with a mentor for a while or working on their own and learning by trial and error. Regardless, it is your job as the trainer to teach them the basic skills for them to be functional. After training, everyone else needs to know they will have to assist the new hire after training. I always tell people that new hire training classes are like Boot Camp to the military. You get the necessary skills and knowledge on how to conduct yourself; then you go off to war! In most industries, it is probably not that drastic (unless you are actually going into the military). After new hire training, you go to the job to learn more specifics about your role and responsibilities. That's how training works. You get trained on some specific or general process then go to perform the job where you learn much more information, processes, systems, networks, etc. Whether you are going to the floor at a Contact Center, the showroom at an auto dealership, or to a hospital emergency department, you get the basics in the classroom, then go on to apply the skills and knowledge learned in the real world after training.

Periodically Check/Test for Understanding and Retention

Since we are discussing periodic checks for understanding and retention, I will ask you a couple of questions right now! I'm glad you have been paying attention while reading this book because it is time for another Pop Quiz! Don't worry, it won't be difficult and is not going to be 100 multiple-choice, True-False, or essay questions. I will take it easy on you and only ask two questions:

- **Question 1:** What is one way to elicit buy-in from the participants in your class?
  Answer: Use real-life stories to relate to and connect with the group. *(See Chapter 4: Soft Skills)*

- **Question 2:** What can you do if you do not know the answer to a question someone asked?
  Answer: Use the Toss Back Method to get the class engaged. Let the group know you do not have the answer, but will place the

question in the Parking Lot, and get the answer to them in a specified and reasonable amount of time.

I told you it wouldn't be too difficult. While you were reading through this material, perhaps you were a little caught off guard by the questions. I hope you were able to answer them, or at least flip back to the chapter or section and find the answers pretty quickly. This is precisely what I want you to do during your training classes. It doesn't have to be too difficult, just throw a couple of questions out there for the class to answer and gauge where they are. If you are already doing this, great! You are right on track or are ahead of the game. If you are thinking, "This is too simple; trainers should be doing this in their training rooms; no one should have to be told to do this." You are right and wrong. The fact is, I have sat in on hundreds of training sessions, and this is something I see overlooked by many trainers. Sometimes it seems the goal is to just get through the material as quickly as possible with no regard to ensure the learners retained any of the information presented. Checking or testing for understanding and retention of the material makes sure everyone is on the same page during the training. Use question and answer, break out, and teach-back sessions to facilitate the learning and see how much information the participants have retained. You can even give them a formal test or quiz. I have some of those built into my courses, as well. It doesn't matter how you facilitate the exercise. As long as you do it, the results will answer the question, "Are they getting it, or do the participants need more review?"

Show Em, Don't Tell Em!

Adult learning principles suggest people learn better when you show them how to do something rather than just telling them the answers. Think about it. If every single time you had a question you came to me and I gave you the answer, would you need to learn how to find the answer? No! You would keep coming back to me to get the answer time and time again. Hopefully, you would remember it, but if you didn't, there would be no incentive to learn how to find the answer.

Do Not Give Them Everything, Teach Them to Fish

Early in my career, I was taught a principle I still follow today. "Do not give your trainees all of the answers; teach them how to fish." Have you heard this classic principle before? If you give a man a fish he will eat for a day; if you teach a man to fish, he will eat for a lifetime. This principle suggests you show people how to be self-sufficient rather than coming to you for the answers whenever they have a question unless that is your intent. Some trainers want their trainees to come to them for everything, and there are reasons for this. Various motives are:

- The trainer is a micro-manager
- The trainer wants everyone to know how smart they are and receive all the credit
- The trainer uses this method as a means of self-preservation (trying to make themselves indispensable.)
- The trainer is new to the role and has not learned to allow their trainees to be autonomous and self-sufficient

Don't be that trainer! There are many reasons you should not operate this way, but I will tell you, I do not follow the methodology of having my staff (or the trainees either for that matter) being totally reliant on me. I consider myself a teacher at my core, so I teach, I guide, I train! I would rather show you how to find information rather than hand you something you could get yourself. What will happen when I am not there to answer the question? The individual may get lost, and that is a great disservice to the person I am supposed to be educating. I would be wasting their time and mine. Besides, by showing people how to fish, I free myself up to be able to work on other things or follow up on tasks I need to complete.

Do They Know Where to Find It?

There is a common misconception out there. People think that they have to learn and memorize **everything** when in training. This is simply not true. After all, they are new to the business, organization, and sometimes new to the industry! I tell my trainees they don't always have to know everything; they just need to know where to find anything. When training, I emphasize to my trainees that I do not want them to stress out and feel like they must memorize everything. When you have a training class that is days or even weeks-long, there is way too much content and too many principles to remember. There are ways to enhance the learning and create resources for the participants to recall

"I would rather teach you to how to find information rather than hand you something you could get yourself."

the information later. One of these ways is to document the information. Documentation is always helpful and can be used to benefit both the instructor and the participants. One of my favorite things to do while training is to record information on wall charts. This information is displayed throughout the training and can be used as reference material. When there are questions from the group, I will often point to the wall charts, if the answers have been recorded there, and allow participants to use them during quizzes as well. I emphasize they do not have to memorize everything; they need to know how to find the information. While some information or answers will be written on wall charts, the charts could merely serve as a reminder of where to find the information in a technical system. I also make sure the participants get in on the action and will often ask for volunteers to record answers from the audience when I facilitate exercises. I also encourage them to take their own notes because some people retain information better when they write things down. This keeps them involved and gives them another opportunity to be stakeholders in their own learning.

CHAPTER 7
WRITING AND DESIGNING TRAINING MATERIAL

Question: Do I have to learn how to create training material if I am a trainer and not an Instructional Designer?

Answer: Yes! Every trainer should know how to design, create, and facilitate their own training material. Not only does it make you a better trainer, but it gives you a deeper connection to the content and the art of training.

This chapter contains information on the following topics:
- **Instructional Design**
- **Break It Up! /Chunking**
- **Activities**
- **Case Studies**
- **Creating an Agenda**
- **Creating a Trainer's Syllabus**

"Of all the life skills available to us, communication is perhaps the most empowering." – Bret Morrison

In 2013, I started a new position with a new company and attended a new hire technical training class. The instructors facilitating the course taught us how to document notes and record information in the patient's Electronic Health Record. There were lots of different templates, plenty of screens, and a ton of mouse clicks to ensure the data was documented correctly. There were handouts passed around for this 12-hour class, facilitated over three days (three four-hour sessions). The handouts consisted of an agenda, usernames and passwords, and some quizzes. Right away, I identified a critical problem with the information distributed to the participants in this class. Some of you may already be thinking about it, where was the training material? Now, this may be fine for people who have photographic memories, but for the rest of us, we need something tangible to hold on to. You know, something to refer back to if you got lost or behind and needed to catch up. Even somewhere to jot down notes would have been great. When I asked the facilitator if they had any training content, they told me they were not allowed to give out the material because it was too expensive to print. They explained that you could take notes on your agenda and would be given paper if you needed to take additional notes. I thought, how am I supposed to remember all of this stuff? Even if I take notes, I will not have a point of reference to know what the notes pertain to! I would not have any screenshots or examples at all. I can draw a little, but not quickly enough to capture the level of detail to make the information relevant and useful. I do not recall who it was, but I remember one of my mentors saying, *"If you* want people to remember something, give them something to take with them." In my experience, I have found, people will appreciate quality training material and refer back to the content you give them. This can be a valuable resource to both the facilitator and trainee alike.

One day, I gave one of my new employees an assignment, let's call him Shawn. I told Shawn we would be assisting a trainer in another department, we will call her Christina, by helping her re-design her training modules and updating it to match our department's design standards. It should have been a simple project. Take the material from the other trainer (which was all in PowerPoint presentations) and convert it to a Word document, add learning exercises, quizzes, and a syllabus. There was no rush on the project, and I advised Shawn to complete the task in between New Hire Training classes and other priorities. After about a few weeks, I checked back in to see the progress on the project. To my surprise, the project was not as far along as I thought it would be. A few weeks should

"If you want people to remember something, give them something to take with them."

have been enough time to make a significant dent in the project. I thought it would have been at least 70 - 75% complete. I soon discovered that instead of him following my instruction of taking the existing material and directly converting it, he was re-creating everything from scratch! I had given the framework for completing the project to Shawn but realized I needed to be more explicit in my instruction. I should have held a meeting with the two trainers and walked them through the process, step by step. This was something that I didn't think was necessary at the time, but in retrospect, I definitely should have completed that action at the beginning of the project. I had to go back to the basics. I went back to Shawn and sat down with him. I discussed the progress on the project and told him I thought he would be further along with the project and why. Shawn said to me that he was a little confused about the direction and how to actually go about completing the project. I started from the top, and we walked through how he would go about completing the assignment. Shawn had completed some learning exercises that were very well put together, and I made sure to compliment him on that work. He said he was stuck on how to organize some of the material, so I walked Shawn through my design process. I knew Shawn was a recent college graduate, so I asked, "How do you write a paper for school?' He said, "First, I create an outline of the discussion topics for the paper, then I fill in the content and add transitional sentences." I replied, "Perfect! Now you are getting it!" I told him, after the transitional sentences, he needed to write the introductions and closings for each module. Then he would also need to add in the learning exercises. Once all of these things were complete, create a syllabus, and estimate the times for the sections and courses. The light bulb went off! Shawn now understood precisely what was expected and exactly how to complete the work. I thought I had been clear in the beginning but realized I needed to sit down and walk him through the process for him to truly get it. Now Shawn had a framework to use on this current project and future content development projects. He learned a transferrable skill that he could duplicate anywhere he went. Shawn felt relieved to learn something new and now knew what to do moving forward. I felt accomplished because I transferred knowledge to Shawn, and he told me he appreciated the information. This experience was a reminder that I must level set with my team on every project until I knew my staff understood the expectations and how to accomplish them before starting a project.

Instructional Design

Designing training material is not as easy as it may seem, but it does not have to be an overwhelming task. Creating systems and standardized processes can make the most difficult tasks simple if the processes are correctly structured. As with any other activity, it depends on what type of document you are creating, and any project can be broken down into smaller steps. Various kinds of Instructional Design training material include but are not limited to:

- Training Manuals
    - Facilitator's Guide
    - Participant's Guide
- Cheat Sheets
- Workflow Process Documents
- Tips of the Week
- Quarterly Update Sheets
- Training Newsletters
- Training Flyers

- Bookmarks
- Online Training Courses
- Training Videos

During a Training Needs Analysis Meeting, the type of training and delivery style needed to support the learning must be decided. Once this is determined, the planning stage of the training design can begin.

Break It Up! /Chunking

No matter the length of the training, you want to break up the class into digestible pieces. This is often referred to in the design as "Chunking." Chunking is generally known as taking smaller bits of information and putting them together in a more significant chunk but the way we use the term is the opposite. Most people can only absorb so much information before they become disengaged or distracted. In other words, people will get bored in your class if your lecture is too long. Your course should include different chunks, activities, and other things to keep the learner Edu-Tained (Educated and Entertained.) A general rule of thumb is to break up your class into 20-minute chunks. To keep it simple, if you are facilitating a one-hour training, you may want to have three 20-minute sections. I would also break up one of those 20-minute sections further to include time for your opening, closing, questions and answer, and an activity. Below is a high-level guideline of how I would structure the time for a 1-hour training session.

"Most people can only absorb so much information before they become disengaged or distracted."

High-Level Training Class Timeline	
• Introduction	5 minutes
• Instruction Section One	20 minutes
• Activity	5 minutes
• Instruction Section Two	20 minutes
• Q & A	5 minutes
• Closing	5 minutes

Figure 7.1 Training Class Timeline

Activities

Activities are an integral part of your training sessions. They should be engaging and always get people involved. They are a mechanism used to get people out of their normal learning pattern and facilitate the learning. As discussed previously, you will have different types of learners in the class, and you will need to appeal to all of the learners. Activities are not only a way to appeal to the Visual and Kinesthetic learners but a way to break up the class and get everyone involved. I like to conduct activities that get people up out of their seats or that allow them to work with other people that are not part of their current group. This encourages teamwork, networking, and meeting new people. When designing or using existing activities, make sure they fit within the time frame of your training sessions. Activities that run too long can cause you to rush through other sections of the training that may be crucial to take your time on.

Case Studies

Case studies are another way to break up the learning and appeal to different learning styles. Case studies allow participants to learn from real-life examples of what the users will go through. The case studies should be directly related to their jobs or situation, so the learners will connect with these types of examples. Case studies can be used as reference material or as an activity. They work well as activities because you can get people to work together in groups and solve a problem presented by a case study. As the trainer, walk around to engage the groups and facilitate the learning. Once the specified time is up, wrap-up the activity by discussing the outcomes and ask how the learners arrived at their conclusions. Case studies work well as self-directed learning activities as well to facilitate and reinforce the training.

On the following pages are two examples of case studies I would include in a participant's training guide. These would be intended as exercises participants would complete individually, in groups, or as an entire class.

Case Study # 1: Product Sales Call

A customer calls in looking for an item they had previously ordered. They don't remember when they ordered it but states they are pretty sure it was sometime last year. They also tell you the product must be from a specific manufacturer but does not remember the name. They want to make sure it was the one they ordered before.

1. What do you do to find the product they are looking for?

2. How do you verify it is the correct product they ordered previously?

3. Where is the order placed?

4. What are the steps to place the order?

_____

_____

_____

_____

_____

_____

Figure 7.2 Case Study Example #1 Product Sales Call

Case Study #2: Documentation in the Electronic Medical Record

A patient calls in to schedule a doctor's appointment for his wife. He says his wife is complaining of having a sore throat and wants to see her doctor as soon as possible. After asking a few questions, you find out the patient's primary doctor is on vacation, and the patient lives in Orange County but is visiting family in Los Angeles. They are willing to see a different doctor.

1. Are you able to schedule the appointment?
2. What information do you need verify to schedule the appointment?
3. Which doctor do you schedule the patient with?
4. What information must you tell the patient to confirm the appointment?

_____

_____

_____

_____

_____

Figure 7.3 Case Study Example #2 Documentation in the Electronic Medical Record

These are just a couple of examples of scenarios or what I call case studies. I use these types of scenarios to get the participants creative juices flowing and to get the class used to the information they will come across in their jobs. Creating examples is easy because the scenarios will be created based on what happens in real life. The scenarios or case studies work well because it allows the participants to solve cases and perform the job in a low-risk environment.

Creating an Agenda

We talked about the importance of creating an agenda in **Chapter 1. Opening the Class: Introductions, Ice Breakers, and Energizers.** The purpose of an agenda is to serve as a high-level roadmap for the class. It is useful to give to your learners because it lets them know the direction the class is going. The agenda will contain the topics to be covered and generally the order of those topics. Now how do you create an agenda? Some debate whether you should create it before designing the training material or after creating the training material. I am going to say I do both. I create a rough draft of my agenda that identifies the topics I want to teach. Then I use my agenda outline to fill in the content. If topics or content needs to be moved around because it does not flow the way I want it to, I adjust and update the agenda. The last thing I do is add timing. I guesstimate how much time I think it will take to cover each section and will tighten those times up during a trial run or the first time I facilitate the class. Like I said earlier, it is entirely up to you whether you want to include the times on the agenda you distribute to the class. If you go over time, just know occasionally, people will bring it up. It shouldn't be a big issue, though, and I want to stress, the times on an agenda are approximate and meant to be a guideline. (Although you will want to stick to exact times on meeting agendas.)

Creating a Trainer's Syllabus

A syllabus is similar to an agenda in that it also contains all of the information included in your agenda. The trainer's syllabus is specifically for the trainer and is not for the participants. This document is beneficial to trainers that are new to training (or new to the subject matter) and existing trainers as well. The difference between the agenda and the syllabus is there is much more detailed information included in the syllabus. The information included in my syllabus will contain the following:

- Training Topics
- Training Objectives
- Pre/Post work the trainer must complete
- Cues for breaks and lunches
- Links to all the additional information like training manuals, handouts, sign-in sheets, videos, instructions for activities, quiz answers, etc.
- Start and Stop times for each section or activity
- The format of the training (Instructor-Led, Self-Paced, Printed Material, Trainee Led, LMS, etc.

I like the syllabus format because anything and everything the trainer needs and could want can be listed there. (Although I guess you could arrange an agenda the same way with the links and additional information. It will be up to you to decide, but I included an example of a syllabus on the next page.

Sample Training Syllabus

AVANT GARDE TRAINING GROUP

Topic	Objective	Format	Material	Time	Min
Day 1					
Preliminary Work	• New Hire Training Material	Printed	• Sign-In Sheet from printed LMS • Usernames Information Sheet • Train Environment Generic Usernames and Passwords • Syllabus • Day 1 Training Assessment Key AM & PM • Technical Training User Manual • Basic Navigation User Manual • Telephone Call Videos • Tent Cards	24 Hours before training	
Complete before Day 1	• Check Test a Environment for Training Functionality	Trainer			
Welcome	• Introductions • Ground rules • Ice Breaker	Instructor Led	• Introductions Document • Ice Breaker of your choice	8:05 am	30 min
Login and Preferences	• Sign in to Production • Change Password • Set System Preferences • Sign in to System Training Environment	Instructor Led	• Nursing Training Manual o Pages 10-15	8:35 am	25 min
Learning Activity	• Set Preferences in Training Environment	Self-Paced	• Nursing Technical Training Manual o Page 16	9:00 am	10 min
Basic Navigation	• Main Tool Bar • Title Bar • Menu Bar • Status Bar • History Bar	Instructor Led	• Nursing Technical Training Manual o Pages 17-22	9:10 am	30 min
Learning Activity: Scavenger Hunt	• Look Up a Patient • History Bar • Review Patient Allergies • Review Patient Medications	Self-Paced	• Nursing Technical Training Manual o Pages 23-24	9:40 am	20 min
AM Break				**10:00 am**	**15 min**
During Training	• Take attendance in Learning Management System (LMS)	Instructor Led	**LMS Instructions**		
Activity Review Scavenger Hunt	• Review the Learning Activity with your class and Check For Understanding.		• Facilitate a Learning Activity	10:15 am	15 min

Figure 7.2 Sample Training Syllabus

CHAPTER 8
TESTS OR REVIEWS FOR UNDERSTANDING

Question: What kind of review should I do? Should I just ask my class random questions from the material?

Answer: Yes, you should ask your class questions. However, there are activities you can facilitate that will keep the participants more involved, which you can use to gauge their level of understanding.

This chapter contains information on the following topics:
- **Tests/Quizzes for Understanding**
- **Reviews for Understanding**
    - Straight Review Activity
    - A-Z Review Activity
    - Teach-Back Review
    - Educational Games (Activities)
- **What Did You Learn Yesterday, This Morning, This Afternoon? Activity**
- **Is more review needed?**

"In learning, you will teach, and in teaching you will learn." – Phil Collins

After you have facilitated your content, you will want an ROI (Return On your Investment.) You want to make sure the learners understood and have retained the information you've given them. There are a couple of ways to do this. You can test, quiz, or review the information with the participants to check their knowledge. These are effective ways to check for retention of the information you delivered to your learners. After all you created the material using your blood, sweat, and tears!

Tests/Quizzes for Understanding

One of the most basic ways to determine if someone is retaining the information you are teaching them is to give them a test or a quiz. You teach the participants a chunk of content and then ask them questions about the subject matter. This can be done verbally, on paper, or electronically. I use a variety of these methods in my training classes, and you should too. Another reason I like tests is that they can provide useful information in terms of tracking data. Results of a test can prompt questions things like:

- Are the participants retaining the information?
- Is the test too difficult?
- Is there something wrong with the test?
- Is the instructor covering all of the correct material?
- Is the instructor just giving the participants the answers and not actually teaching them the content?

"You can test, quiz, or review the information with the participants to check their knowledge."

There are advantages and disadvantages to each method of testing listed in the chart below:

Types of Tests	Advantages	Disadvantages
Verbal	• Easy to administer on the fly • Some audience participation • Immediate Feedback	• No data or record-keeping • May not get 100% class participation • Questions may not be standardized
Paper	• Questions are pre-determined • Will have a written record of test • 100% class participation • Good for data gathering	• Have to make copies/kill trees • Must have covered material on the test • Have to grade tests, which takes time • May or may not have immediate feedback
Electronic	• The system can auto-grade tests • Immediate feedback • Great for documentation • Can be auto-assigned to learners • Great for data gathering	• Must have covered material on the test • May have occasional system issues • Have to address users who do not pass the test individually

Figure 8.1 Advantages/Disadvantages to Different Types of Tests

As you can see from the previous example, there are a few things to think about when determining which type of test or quiz to administer during your trainings. They are all relatively easy to create and manage but have subtle differences that must be considered depending on the type of training you plan to conduct. You may prefer to use verbal tests for brief informal training classes that discuss high-level concepts, like Soft Skills Training for instance, where you may not need to keep a record of test scores. You may have a Technical Training class where trainees must learn strict concepts, standards, regulations, etc. that require a 95% test score pass rate. In this example, you may want to give a rigorous, in-depth assessment electronically, so you have access to all the necessary data needed to report information on tracking, trending, and compliance. This is not a hard and fast rule that is set in stone, though. You may want to give a more rigorous comprehensive test for Soft Skills Training and choose to provide verbal mini-quizzes in a Technical Training class. The question you have to ask yourself is, "What is my expected outcome from giving this test, and what am I going to do with the results?"

1. Am I just checking to make sure the class is with me, or am I confirming the transfer of knowledge is complete?
2. Do I need to keep records of the results of this test to report to senior leadership?
3. Do I need data to validate the test is appropriate for the training content?

The answer to these and similar questions will usually determine which type of test or quiz you want to give to the participants.

Reviews for Understanding

Reviews are an essential part of testing for the learner's understanding and can be fun exercises as well. These can include breakout sessions, teach-backs, questions and answers, and other activities.

Listed below are four review exercises that I've learned. They will test your learners' understanding and make your classes more engaging for the participants. These are not dull lecture reviews but are activities meant to be interactive and involve everyone. Some of the reviews I like are listed as follows:

- Straight Review Activity
- A-Z Review Activity
- Teach-Back Review Activity
- Educational Games (Activities)

Straight Review Activity

One type of review I like to use is easy to use and very straightforward. I ask the participants to tell me one thing they learned during the session. It can serve as a review after a section at the end of the day or first thing in the morning. I occasionally use a straight review as an ice-breaker after lunch or first thing in the morning to jog the participants' memories and get their informational juices flowing. If they give me a one- or two-word answer, I always follow up on the initial question with an additional question that asks them to take a deeper dive. I want them to explain why it is important and why the information matters to them. A simple question like "What did you learn yesterday? Or what were the key points we discussed today?" keeps the participants on their toes, especially when they are expecting me to ask them. To get the class up and involved, I sometimes ask people to get out of their seats and come up to the wall chart and write down their responses. The great thing about this is these wall charts will serve as open resources for their mid-class or end of class tests. In my training classes, participants are not required to memorize everything but instead become an expert at finding the information and are required to use **every** resource available to them.

Figure 8.2 Straight Review Activity (What Did You Learn Today) Wall Chart Example

A-Z Activity

The A-Z activity is a simple exercise where you write the alphabet in two columns on a large wall chart. (A-M and N-Z.) On the left side, starting at the top of the paper, you'll write out the individual letters A-M (The letter A at the top and ending with the letter M at the bottom of the page. In the top center of the page, with the individual letters N-Z (The letter N at the top/center and Z at the bottom/center. Have the participants come up with a word related to the terms and actions they have learned during the lesson that starts with each letter of the alphabet. It may be challenging to come up with some of the words, for example, words that begin with the letters Q, X, or Z, so they may have to be creative. They can use words that contain the letter, meaning they do not have to start with the letter. *(See Figure 8.3 A-Z Activity Example on the next page)* As the facilitator, you will want to come up with a list of words in advance in case they get stuck that will enable you to help them out. The A-Z exercise helps to jog their memories about what they learned. You will leave the wall charts up to assist them with retention of information and assist when they are taking quizzes. In adult learning, I often remind people adult learning is not like school where they must memorize everything, as long as they know where to find the information, they hold the keys to success. Participants often shared with me the wall charts helped them to remember the answers long after they completed training because the charts were ingrained in their memory.

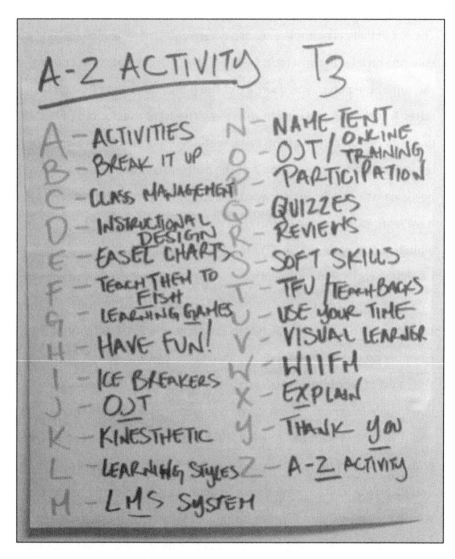

Figure 8.3 A-Z Activity Wall Chart Example

Teach-Back Review Activity

In **CHAPTER 6: FACILITATION TECHNIQUES & MORE**, I explained Teach-Backs are by far my favorite activity to facilitate while in a class. I believe if you can teach something, then you truly learned and understood what you were taught. In this exercise, I split the class into groups then give them topics to review and teach-back to the rest of the group. I allow them to use whatever presentation method they would like. PowerPoint, wall charts, storyboards, educational games, lectures, or any other means of presentation are acceptable. If the group (all members of the group must contribute and present) can demonstrate they understand the subject matter, the exercise tends to be a successful one. As the participants present on their topic, I am there as a resource to fact check, correct, clarify or expand on information needed during the presentation. Teach-backs are a fun activity to use as a quick review or a culmination of a class, and the participants usually like to showcase how much they know. Some groups get incredibly creative with their presentations, and I allow them to go for it within the allotted time frame.

Educational Games (Activities)

Educational games can be a great and exciting way to review information, as we discussed in **Chapter 3: Making Training Fun**. What better way to review information than to have a fun activity to reinforce what was learned earlier in the day or at the end of the class. These have always been a big hit in my experience.

What Did You Learn? (Yesterday, This Morning, This Afternoon) *Activity*

The next exercise is one that works at any time of the day. I often use this activity as a warm-up at the beginning of the day, a warm-up just after a lunch break or a cool down at the end of the day. I like it because the purpose is two-fold:

1. The exercise can be used as an ice-breaker first thing in the morning to jog the memory of the learners to review and recall what information was covered in the class the day before
2. The exercise can be used as a review at the end of the day to show the learners how much we accomplished during the session and how much they recalled.

Depending on the size of the class, I will start the exercise by asking the learners to tell me one or two things they learned about a particular session or from the day before, without looking at their notes. I do this to give me an idea of how much they recalled from their memory. This tells me which topics I need to cover more in-depth and what content I don't have to worry about. Each individual must provide a different answer or topic to ensure they all engage in the exercise. I record everything on wall charts and ask the participants probing questions to expand on more complicated subjects as I continue. I leave the wall charts up to allow the participants to use them as resources later in the class. If someone asks a question and the answer is listed on a wall chart, I refer them to the wall, teaching them to use all of their available resources before they ask a question. Even in a question, there is a lesson.

Is More Review Needed?

A trainer once asked me, "If I am delivering the subject matter, facilitating exercises, educational games, and quizzes, how many reviews should I do? "The answer is simple; you should review as much as necessary. Some trainers find this answer hard to digest because they are looking for a more definitive answer derived from a mathematical equation or specific training to review ratio. Well, I'm sure someone out there has probably created one, but I haven't found it yet nor have I looked. (Hmm, maybe I should create one.) However; I do ensure that I have built a curriculum that:

- Contains multiple learning/teaching styles
- Thoroughly reviews the material
- Engages the participants to ensure they have digested and understood the concepts and information

That's it, that's my formula. I build reviews into the training material and arrange the course to include multiple styles and ways to review the material.

Now, after all of that there will be people in your classes who still won't get it. Even after you have gone through all of the material in your training manual, everything that you had in your skillset, after you have used all of the tools in your toolkit, and after you have pulled all of your tricks out of your top hat; they still don't get it. These are the people who you must sit down and have a conversation with. The purpose of this discussion is to find out if there is anything you can do differently to help them understand. It may also be to help them determine if this is the right fit for them professionally at this time. I have had those conversations, and they are not always easy, but they are necessary. You never want to set someone up for failure and send them out unprepared. Especially if it is an industry where sending someone out to the field that couldn't pass training could be dangerous. In an industry like healthcare, patient safety could be at risk and is different than other industries where someone may have to wait a few extra minutes for their cheeseburger or a larger sized basketball shoe. They all matter; and here is the point. I would prefer not to send someone out of training when they have not grasped the fundamental or critical elements of the job they are about to perform. Knowing they may become responsible for losing the company money or worse, causing someone harm does not sit well with me.

Call Confirmation Review

Let's discuss an example of how I reviewed with trainees at a Contact Center. I frequently trained new hire classes for agents whose job was to take calls for patients who wanted to schedule doctor's appointments. At the end of the phone call, they were required to confirm the visit. They were responsible for giving the patient the following four pieces of information to the patient:

- The name of the doctor they would be seeing

- The reason for the visit or why they were making the appointment
- The date and time of the appointment
- Advising the patient to arrive fifteen minutes before the appointment time to check-in.

The confirmation was a key driver for the call to remind the patient of what was discussed and to ensure everything was documented correctly. This sounds like an easy thing to do; after all, there were only four things to confirm, and it was right on the screen in front of them, but it did not always go as planned. While we role played taking calls, the funniest thing would happen, the trainees would forget details of the call confirmation or forget to confirm the call entirely! While this was okay in training, it would not be when they got to the floor, so what I did was simple. I had them take mock calls, make mock appointments, and confirm the appointments with each other until they were sick of it. The participants would all say they had it down and didn't need to practice or review anymore. I had them take turns confirming the call in front of the class, and without fail, the person who insisted the most that they did not need to practice would forget one of the details. I would make the entire class confirm again. I felt like a basketball or football coach that made the team run laps when one person messed up a drill. They repeated this exercise so much, one trainee told me her husband said he knew how to verify a call because she was confirming appointments in her sleep! It may be funny or irritating depending on which side of the coin you are on, but everyone that came out of my class had the concepts down, especially confirming calls. Role-playing is just another type of review you can use to help learners retain information, and this example answers the question of how much review is needed? Again, the answer is simple, as much review as is required or until they are confirming calls in their sleep!

CHAPTER 9
SUPER USERS, E-LEARNING, AND SELF-PACED LEARNING

Question: What do I do if I have a large number of people to train, and Instructor-Led Training is not an option?

Answer: There are a few things you can do. Options include; facilitating a live online session, having the participants take self-directed online e-Learning, or use Super Users to facilitate the class.

This chapter contains information on the following topics:
- Super Users
- E-Learning
- Live Online Sessions
- Self-Paced Online Courses (LMS Courses)
- Pre-Recorded Online Training Sessions
- Read and Confirm (Attestations)

"The beautiful thing about learning is that no one can take it away from you." – B.B. King

Super Users

I briefly mentioned Super Users in an earlier chapter but did not really explain or elaborate on who they are and what they do. Super Users are not a form of E-Learning, but I thought the concept of the Super User fit in this chapter because they can be utilized as a facilitator when you are not able to be physically present for training. For example, you may have large-scale organization-wide training but only have a small training team. In this case, you will need people to support your training team.

A Super User is a Subject Matter Expert that is very familiar with the content, processes, and inner workings of a job or industry. They are often referred to as Leads in the department and have more knowledge than many of the workers in their division or work unit. Usually, Super Users do not hold an official leadership position or title, but they may if your organization has created an official title for them. In my experience, Super Users have been utilized to assist with things like documentation of processes, user acceptance testing, short term supervision, and of course, training. This training can be both in-class or on-the-job and are a valuable resource to the training team.

"A Super User is a Subject Matter Expert that is very familiar with the content, processes and inner workings of a job or industry."

In instances where there is a large group to train, and the training team cannot reach everyone, Super Users can conduct some of the trainings. The training team will need to build a curriculum to conduct a T3 or Train the Trainer session so the

Super Users learn the content trained and what the expectations will be. Also, make sure to give them a syllabus for the class to ensure consistency within the training.

Super Users are a valuable resource to any training department and should be compensated for the work they do outside of their regular work duties. How and when should be decided by the training team and or management group. Earlier in my career, I served as a SME or Super User and was compensated in several ways. I received monetary bonuses, tickets to attend sporting events, lunch or dinner with the leadership team, comp: time off, selection of better work hours, and other things. As a staff member, I saw these opportunities as a chance to better myself, showcase my skills, and expand my network. It allowed me to do something different than I usually did every day. When recruiting for Super Users or starting a Super User program, the opportunities mentioned above should be some of your selling points to your staff. Participation in the Super User Program should also be voluntary because you want people who are invested and who actually want to perform the functions to be a part of the program.

E-Learning

I'm almost certain you already know what an e-Learning is, but you know what happens when you assume, so I will briefly explain. E-Learning stands for Electronic Learning, and it is pretty standard in most organizations. If you have ever taken an online class at school or work, you have participated in a version of e-Learning. So why would you want to train anyone online? There are various reasons you may choose to teach them online or electronically:

- You need to facilitate training for a large number of people but are not be able to get them all in an instructor-led training.
- You may have to train the staff on a very tight timeline or have a deadline that is non-conducive to yours or the participants' schedules.
- The people you need to train are in multiple locations across the city, state, country, or world even!

Live Online Training Sessions

Successful online training is a facilitation style that is suited for a more advanced facilitator; because of the potential for many distractions on the part of the learner. However, facilitators can learn to master this type of training and deliver presentations that the participants will enjoy and remember. WebEx is a tool that I have used to facilitate online training, but there are several platforms out there that work just as well. WebEx, Skype, Zoom, GoToMeeting, Google Hangout Meet are platforms that are used for online presentations. I have not used all of these presentation platforms but do your homework, and you will be able to pick the right one for your needs. Some of them are low or no cost options, and the results may vary depending on your needs. I am most familiar with WebEx, so I will reference it in my following example.

A skilled facilitator can perform a masterful online training session using WebEx or any other online training platform. There are tools within this system that can be used to make your online training fun and engaging. Good trainers will use the tools accessible to them in the online training software like:

- Q&A Sessions
- Mini-quizzes
- Hand Raise feature
- Polling or survey feature
- Highlighter feature
- Pen feature
- Chat box

WebEx is useful for class registration, attendance tracking reporting, and you can even record the training session for use at a later date for people to access if they missed the training. WebEx can be set up to send out reminder email notifications to the participants, and trainer, so they do not forget when the training is scheduled.

Here are ten tips to help facilitate online training:

1. Conduct the training in a quiet space to minimize background noise or distractions.
2. Use two computer monitors to help facilitate the training more easily. You can run the presentation on one screen and handle any administrative duties on the other. (Managing attendance or display of quiz questions, talking points, facilitation notes, etc.)
3. Make sure to prepare well in advance and have all of your reference material handy.

4. Correctly set up the class and do not to forget your attendance and data tracking information.
5. Display your Welcome Slide five minutes before the class starts so people will have background information on the course while they wait.
6. Don't skimp on the quality of the training material.
7. Exert the same amount of energy, if not more, into an online as to do into a live training. Though the participants cannot see you, they will hear you, and you want to have that same energy as if they were right there in the room with you.
8. Remember to use an agenda, participation tools, trainer contact information, thank you screen, etc.
9. Make sure the timing is correct
10. If needed, send out your quizzes, certificates, and after class surveys through the LMS System, so you have a record of valuable data analytics for tracking, trending, and feedback purposes.

Self-Paced Online Courses (LMS Courses)

LMS stands for Learning Management System and is where many training organizations house or store their electronic training material. It is also where participants can go to access this information at any time. LMS courses are helpful because the sessions are conducted online and do not need an instructor to be present. Self-paced online courses can be taken alone by the user on their own time and at their own speed. Many organizations use their LMS Systems to deliver mandatory quarterly or annual training driven by regulatory requirements. This can be very cost and time-effective. Most companies do not want to compensate for lost time, travel expenses, and wages for temporary help to fill in while workers are in training. Another benefit is to those employees who work from home or have access to the system from home. They can access the training anytime, anywhere, again saving time and money. If you have an LMS System at your place of business or have taken an online college course, you may have experienced an LMS System. You might have uploaded an assignment or posted a comment to a chat box using some of the following LMS systems:

- Moodle
- Blackboard
- Docebo
- iSpring Suite
- Adobe
- Cornerstone
- LearnedUpon Limited

I have used a few of these, but not all of them, so you will have to do some research to find out which platform will work best for you.

Now that you know the benefits of conducting online training, let's talk about how to set up one. It's not too difficult, and once you have created a few, you will be able to create these types of trainings quickly. Here is where your instructional design skills are useful. There are many formats you can use to build your online classes. I use PowerPoint to start most of the time because it is easy and what I am most familiar with; however, there are various options. Some tools you can use to create great content are:

- Articulate
- Adobe Captivate
- Camtasia
- Doodly
- Cam Studio
- ScreenFlow
- Free Studio
- Prezi
- Snagit

What you can create with the different software varies, and so do the prices, so you will have to do your research on which software will work for you. There are no right or wrong options here. It is entirely up to you and your budget how you decide to produce your training content and which tools you use to create your courses.

Another consideration you may have before creating the content, if using an LMS System, is to make sure the software is compliant with the LMS System you currently have. It would be disappointing to create all of this great content only to learn that you cannot upload it to your LMS. Most software is shareable across most platforms, so it should not be an issue, but I thought I'd mention it just in case. When creating an online training course, you will want to create a template or general guideline to follow to ensure most of your training is uniform and positioned for success.

GENERAL GUIDELINE FOR ONLINE TRAINING MODULE CREATION
1. Select or locate your LMS System
2. Pick a training design compliant tool to create or load the training into
3. Choose material creation software
4. Pick a presentation tool
5. Create the training content
6. Make sure you have informational tools like *Welcome screen, Agenda, Trainer Contact Information, Thank You Slide, etc.*
7. Make sure the timing is correct
8. Attach your quizzes, certificates and after class surveys
9. Upload training module to the LMS

Figure 9.1 General Guideline for Online Training Module Creation

An important thing to remember is to create and distribute detailed instructions on how to find the course you uploaded to the LMS system. You will waste time and effort replying to emails from users trying to find your course. Trust me, I've been there.

Pre-Recorded Online Training Sessions

When you are facilitating a live-online training course, you may want to record it for future use. Pre-recorded training sessions can be set up to be interactive, similar to the live training sessions. However, since they are not in real-time, there will be different benefits, challenges, and opportunities. One of the differences is that the participants will not be able to ask the facilitator a question or make a comment for clarification on a question. The facilitator will not be able to give extensive real-time feedback or interact with the participants. The training session can include some of the tools used in the live session (but not all), and the input will be limited to pre-determined questions and answers. The facilitator would have to anticipate the questions a participant might have and include those answers in the session and could also add additional reference material for review. Good trainers will use the tools accessible to them with their online training like:

- Q&A Sessions
- Mini and full-length quizzes
- Links to training manuals and user guides
- Links to additional training or reference materials and documents
- Certificates of completion
- Completion Badges

Online training sessions can also include class registration, attendance tracking reporting, and email notifications.

Read and Confirm (Attestations)

What do you do when you have a small amount of information that needs to be delivered to a large group of people in a short amount of time? An option is to have the learners read and attest to understanding the information given to them. Let me be clear; I would not quite call the action of reading and attesting to understanding a document "training" per se; however, sometimes it is the only option for a quick transfer of knowledge, distribution of information, and record keeping of the activity.

The healthcare industry is highly regulated. These rules and regulations must be adhered to; if not, the health plan, provider, or facility can and will be fined heavily depending on the severity of the offense. The staff of these organizations must be adequately trained, not only to avoid those fines but to provide care for the patients in their charge appropriately. Sometimes health plans or health care facilities are audited, and the results of the audit require corrective action. This may require a simple document to be read and understood by the staff in response to that corrective action plan to ensure patient safety. Once read, the user can sign and attest (electronically or on paper) that they have read and understood the document. Once all the participants have completed reading and confirming that they have read the document, then a comprehensive report of all the users who have completed the training activity can be created. A copy of the training completion report can then be sent to the health plan to verify that the staff has been trained and understands the information required. The best way to design this training is electronically through a Learning Management System. The user can access the information, read the information then click a button to confirm understanding. (Usually, the button would be labeled "I Attest." Clicking the button will send the data to a database that can be used later to aggregate the data and produce completion reports to send off to the governing entity.

I usually create this type of training when:

- In response to a regulatory requirement that must be completed with a short timeline
- There is a minimal amount of information required, and it does not require in-person or face-to-face instruction. (Usually one or two pages of information)

Depending on the situation, I will then either create an online training module for future staff to use or add the training content to an existing new hire training curriculum.

CHAPTER 10
CLOSING THE CLASS

Question: *Isn't the class finished when everyone takes their quiz and leaves?*

Answer: *Yes, and no. You want everyone to complete the end of class quiz or survey, but you also want to ensure to close your class properly. You must make sure everyone received the information needed (or knows you will follow up with them). They should also know the next steps after leaving the class, and lastly, you must thank them for coming.*

This chapter contains information on the following topics:

- **Final Reviews and Quizzes**
- **Contact Information**
- **Thank the Participants for Coming**

"The freedom to do your best means nothing unless you are willing to do your best." – General Colin Powell

Final Reviews and Quizzes

Reviews and quizzes are a critical part of learning. They are one way to measure the success of your training. At the end of the class you want to be able to answer questions like:

- *Did the learners understand what you were trying to teach them?*
- *Did the learners retain the information after completing the training?*
- *Is there information not being grasped by the learners, and if so, is it just one person, or is the entire class not getting it?*

Quizzes and tests can answer all of those questions and are just one way to measure the success of the training. The scores can indicate how the class is going and how the trainees are doing. I suggest you conduct a final review before you take a final exam or quiz to end the course. In **Chapter 8: Reviews and Tests for Understanding,** I introduced you to different types of reviews. We discussed review activities like the: Straight Review, A-Z Review, Teach-Back Review, and Educational Games (I mean Activities!).

A Straight Review or Educational Game/Activity can both serve as a perfect end of class review and preparation for the final exam. If you facilitated an educational game previously, this could give the participants a chance to redeem themselves from earlier games. By the end of the course, their knowledge level should be elevated. The

"Quizzes and tests and are just one way to measure success of the training."

games will be more fun because they will have retained much more information since the first time they played them. You can set up the teams the same as before for a rematch or mix up the people in the class to make new teams. Either way, the educational game review should serve as a way to prepare the trainees for the final exam or as a retention tool to close the class out on a high note!

Contact Information

If the participants want to follow up with you or get in touch with you on a later date, they will need your contact information. Telephone numbers, email addresses, and website addresses are all great resources for people to get in touch with you. Make sure to have business cards to hand out (digital or a paper business card) or a slide with your contact information displayed at the end of the course. If you used an Introduction Slide at the beginning of the class and included your contact information on it, use the same one. (No need to re-invent the wheel.) *(See figure 1.8 Class Introduction slide from* **Chapter 1: Opening the Class: Introductions, Ice Breakers, and Energizers)**
The participants can write your information down or take a picture of the slide on their phones with your contact info. This can be extremely helpful to you and the participants, especially if you have your own training or consulting business. In fact, you may want to have a sign-in sheet to collect the participants' information. This way, you can send them a thank you note, or email and any follow-up information promised. If you have your own business, this will be particularly useful

data to add to your contact list and to use for marketing purposes at a later date.

Figure 10.1 Sample Contact Information Slide

Thank the Participants for Coming

Sometimes we forget that the simple things can make the most significant difference in a person's life. What we think is trivial could be very important to another person. In training, one of those simple things is to thank the participants for coming. If I have a presentation, I make sure to include a thank you slide in the slide deck, and I also thank them verbally for participating. Depending on the class, I may send them a thank you note, card, or email. In this communication, I may include information about upcoming classes or other services I have to offer. I also include my contact information, so they know how to get in touch with me. I often get feedback that this small gesture is much appreciated.

Figure 10.2 Sample Thank you Slide

EPILOGUE:
DID I ANSWER ALL OF YOUR QUESTIONS?

Did you think I would leave you without giving you answers to some of the tough questions? Not a chance! Remember those survey questions I asked my new trainers before I conducted their Best Practices session? Let's take a little time to elaborate and reiterate some of those scenarios.

- What do I do with difficult participants like Know It All's?
- How do I handle people in the class who know more than I do about the subject matter?
- What do I do if I don't know the answer to the question I'm being asked?
- How do I stay on track in the classroom?
- What is a Trainer's Toolkit, and what are the things that go into it?
- What should I do with participants who arrive late?
- How do I handle situations when the equipment has technical issues?

"I hated every minute of training, but I said, don't quit. Suffer now and live the rest of your life as a champion." – Muhammed Ali

QUESTION 1

What do I do with difficult participants like Know It All's?

Have the *Know It All* demonstrate the correct way to do things. If they know how to do so, great! If they do not know how, this is also great! It will be an opportunity to teach them something. If the *Know It All* demonstrates an understanding of the information, it will make them feel good that they were able to show everyone. If the Know It All is not able to demonstrate the knowledge correctly, they usually will pipe down and stop bothering you. At least they will stop interrupting the class, which works in your favor! It doesn't mean you are trying to show them up or be rude. You are only allowing the "Know it All" the opportunity to showcase their knowledge. If they are not able to produce, it is a non-confrontational way to ask them to be quiet. It also keeps the situation from turning into a "you versus them" situation. Again, you are merely allowing them to showcase their skills, which either way, you will use to your advantage. Remember, it is all in how you frame it.

Turn them from your foe to your helper and have them drive for you during the class. This way, they get to satisfy their urge to be right all of the time, and you get to have someone that is a subject matter expert on your side, assisting you in the class.

QUESTION 2

How do I handle people in the class who know more than I do about the subject matter?

Sometimes you will have people in your class who have more institutional knowledge than you do. These folks can be similar to but are slightly different than your "Know It All's." They may have been employed by the organization much longer than you and performing their job for years, and that's great. There is nothing wrong with that. However; this presents a different type of challenge, which is why you need to be on top of your game. You do not have to know more than them for you to be able to teach them something. Let's say you are facilitating a class on a new software update, new customer service techniques, or a refresher class on information that is not new at all. If you have people in your class that are very intimate with the subject matter, use them as your Subject Matter Experts. You can use their institutional knowledge to turn then from a disruptor to a helper. Most people love to showcase how much they know, and that can work to your advantage, much like the Know It All. You can turn a potential antagonist into a protagonist who will help others in the class to buy into what you are trying to teach them. If you find yourself in this type of situation, make sure to let the class know that you are not the expert but are there to give them the updates or refresh them on the subject matter (whatever the case may be.) They may try and argue with you about the changes or the process and tell you everything they do not like about it. They may even let you know that they know more than you about the subject matter, but that is not why you are facilitating the class. You have a goal, and that goal is to deliver the information. If they have any issue with the changes, invite them to have that discussion with their leadership. Do not argue with participants. If you do, it will make you look bad, and you will lose every time. Remember, you are a professional trainer and must maintain your poise and composure.

When you get to a point in the class where a participant has more context or information, find out exactly what they know about the subject matter and strategically ask them to share with the class. Ask them how things are handled, processed, or completed. Sometimes, historical context and information can be a valuable resource. This is when you can leverage their knowledge and expertise to your advantage. Make sure the information aligns with the message you are trying to convey. When done properly, you can obtain a powerful ally and maybe even learn something in the process. This person may later sing your praises and tell everyone how much they enjoyed your class. (Because they were able to participate in the teaching and felt connected.) Just remember, when you get new information from a participant, make sure to validate or fact check it for accuracy before passing that information along in any future communications. You should also make a mental note or document it for future use. This process increases your knowledge on that subject; then, you can use it in future trainings.

QUESTION 3

What do I do if I don't know the answer to the question I'm being asked?

There are a couple of ways to address the issue gracefully, and not look like you are incompetent if you don't know the answer to a question a participant has asked you.

The first thing you can do is also the easiest thing to do, tell them you don't know! There is no shame in telling someone you don't know something (unless you say "I don't know" to every question they ask. Then you lose credibility.) Advise the participant that you will follow up on their question and get back to them with the answer. Sometimes, there are process changes in progress within the organization, and all of the details are not finite yet, though there are changes that will affect the workforce. In this case, more information will come at a later date, but the people performing the job will need to receive an update. There have been countless instances when there were changes made, and I had to train on processes not yet fully developed. It is okay to tell the participants as long as you are not framing it negatively. For example, "Yeah, management doesn't know what they are doing. We are building the plane while we are flying it!" No, you don't want to say things like that because you will lose your participants and damage your credibility. Explain that there was an immediate change that happened, and there will be more details to come soon.

The second thing you can do is to put the question in the Parking Lot. A Parking Lot is a great place to put unanswered questions. It is a place to "park" those questions you do not immediately have the answers to or that do not fit within the module you are currently training. This method or tool can be used throughout the training.

Put a Parking Lot Chart on the wall at the beginning of the class. Explain to your participants this is the place you will "Park" the questions you do not have the answers to or that will be answered later on during the session. This tends to work well for people who do not feel comfortable asking their questions in front of everyone in the class. During the break, lunch, or the end of the session, collect all of the questions in the parking lot to see if you can then answer them, have already answered them, or need to answer them at a later time. The key here is the follow-up. A good rule of thumb is to follow-up the same day or within 24 hours. If the participants are coming back to you the next day, then try to answer those questions the following morning. I can't say it enough; the key is to **follow-up**. One of the quickest ways to lose credibility is to tell someone you are going to get back with them and fail to do so.

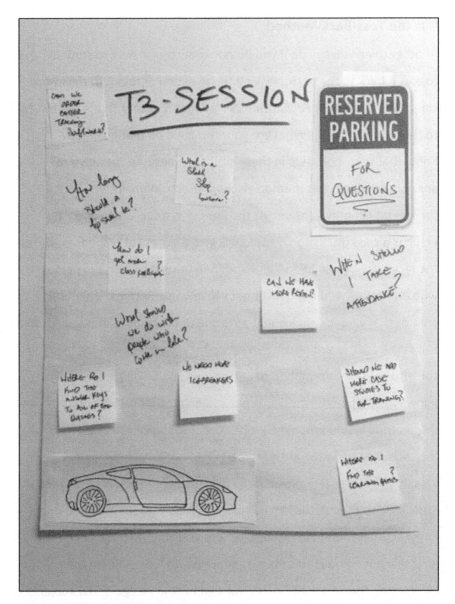

Figure 11.1 Parking Lot Wall Chart Example

Use the Toss-Back Method

Another thing you can do if you do not know the answer to something is to toss it back to the person asking the question or toss it to the entire class. *(See Chapter 6: Facilitation Techniques & More)* That's right; turn to the group and ask, "What are your thoughts on that question?" Know-it-alls are a big help in these situations because they love to answer questions. This method also works exceptionally well when there is no definitive answer, or the answer is a subjective one. The result is a class discussion. People will give a variety of responses, you as the facilitator can build on them and then bring it back to the person who originally asked the question for follow up. Because it generally creates that valuable dialogue, this is one of my favorite methods in Soft Skills classes. The audience's responses may jog your memory, and you can also use this information to add to your toolkit or your wealth of knowledge. When the answer is not subjective or is very technical, then this method would probably not be your first choice; although people in the class may know the answer, you would not be able to verify the validity of the answer immediately. Also, be careful not to overuse the Toss Back Method because participants will start to think you do not know anything and then disengage from you and the class. I once had an instructor who did this every time we asked a question in their class. We quickly discovered the instructor had no knowledge of the subject matter and they lost all credibility with us.

QUESTION 4

How do I stay on track in the classroom?

I love this question because sometimes it is not as easy as it sounds to stay on track in the classroom. (Most trainers are very talkative!) Sometimes people have a lot of questions, or there may be system difficulties, but the basic answer to this question is always to have an agenda or a syllabus for your course. This way, you know where you are supposed to be, how long sections are supposed to take and can speed up or slow down based on where you are in the class.

As part of managing a training department, I like to either pop into a class that is in progress or have one of my leads or supervisors do so to check on the trainers. For new trainers, I check in with them more often at the beginning of their tenure. I like to make sure I am providing my support and make sure they are on track with our training program. For established trainers, I also want to show my support for them and keep them on their toes. Sometimes I use these opportunities to take notes and give feedback as well as share what trainers are doing well in their classrooms with the other trainers during staff meetings. It is a great way to share best practices, tips, tricks, and publicly acknowledge people for a job well done. When I am in the class, I ensure to bring an agenda; this way, I know where the class is and where they are supposed to be. Let me reiterate; it is always best practice to have an agenda or a syllabus. As the old saying goes, *"If you fail to plan, you plan to fail."* Creating a plan or roadmap is genuinely something that should be covered in a Training 101 class. An agenda is a fundamental tool that will help all trainers at any level. When training, participants in your class will ask you questions like:

- What should I expect in this session?
- What subject matter will be covered, or which subject is coming up next?
- What time is the break scheduled?
- How long does this training last?
- Wait, which section are we on?

At some point while you are facilitating, someone in your class will eventually get lost! Would you rather them stop the entire class to ask, "Which section are we reviewing?" or be able to glance at an agenda and find it themselves? I vote for the latter. Whether I am facilitating a four-hour class or a four-week class, I make sure to have an agenda, so people will know exactly what we are covering during the session. If you want to take it a step further, you could include the exact time or time frames you will be facilitating the topics. You will want to be careful about doing this, though, because if you include times and timeframes, the participants will hold you to them. There is always one person that will stop you and point out the fact that you are behind! I always give the class a disclaimer at the beginning that times are approximate, are to be used as a guideline, and I will adjust accordingly. Especially If I know, I may get a little off track during a session. This buys me a little flexibility and lets the "timekeepers" know that I am aware of the time and where we should be in the curriculum.

TRAINING AGENDA TEMPLATE

DAY ONE – CUSTOMER NAVIGATION TRAINING

System: Avant Garde Customer Records (AGCR)
Trainer: Rachel Lozano
Date: 10/1/2019
Time: 8:00 am – 5:00 pm
Location: Training Room 1

AGENDA:

TIME	TOPIC	DETAILS
8:05 AM – 8:35 AM	Welcome	• Ice Breaker • Introductions • Ground Rules
8:35 AM – 9:00 AM	Login and Preferences	• Sign in to Production • Change Password • Set System Preferences • Sign in to System Training Environment
9:00 AM – 9:10 AM	Learning Activity	• Set Preferences in Training Environment
9:10AM – 9:40 AM	Menu Toolbar	• Main Tool Bar • Title Bar • Menu Bar • Status Bar • History Bar
9:40AM – 10:00 AM	Learning Activity: Scavenger Hunt	• Look Up a Customer • History Bar • Customer Orders • Customer Frequent Items • Predictive Pattern/Suggestions
10:00AM – 10:15 AM		15 Minute Break
10:15 AM – 11:30 AM	Scavenger Hunt Review	• Review the Learning Activity with your class and Check for Understanding.
11:30 AM – 12:00 PM	Knowledge Check	• Teach Back
12:00 PM – 1:00 PM		LUNCH
1:00 PM – 3:00 PM	Template Navigation	• Break Out Session
3:00 PM – 3:15 PM		15 Minute Break
3:15 PM – 4:00 PM	Review	• Basic Navigation • Login and Preferences • Menu Toolbar • Template Navigation
4:00 PM – 4:45 PM	Skill Proficiency Assessment	• Day One Test
4:45 PM – 5:00 PM		Wrap Up

Figure 11.2 Sample Training Agenda

QUESTION 5

What is a Trainer's Toolkit, and what are the things that go into it?

Every successful trainer arrives to their training sessions prepared. Part of that preparation includes various items that you will use to facilitate that training. Things that go into your trainer's toolkit depends on the type of training you are going to facilitate. This is not an all-encompassing list; however, I generally will keep most of the items below in my toolkit:

- Clicker
- Ink Pens
- Easel Charts
- Projector
- Flash drive
- Markers
- Notebooks
- Real-Life Stories
- Laptop
- Mouse
- Batteries
- Business Cards
- Speakers/Soundbar
- Hand Sanitizer

QUESTION 6

What should I do with participants who arrive late?

The answer to this will vary according to your guidelines, standards, and company culture. Yup, company culture can sometimes dictate how you handle situations in your training department. The best thing to do is to understand what the company culture is and have a discussion with your leadership and human resources to agree regarding attendance and discipline. I have worked in organizations with strict attendance policies where if you were more than five minutes late, you would be denied entry to the training class and in organizations with lax policies where people seemed to come and go as freely as they liked. It can be easy for a facilitator to "catch someone up" if they have a small class, and the participant arrives a few minutes late. It can also be challenging if there is a large class and you are in the middle of technical training where there may be a ton of content missed. Having to go back is disruptive and unfair to the rest of the group, especially if everyone else showed up on time. Because of this, I decided to establish attendance guidelines at my last organization. Our policy was designed to mitigate any situations with tardiness. Therefore, I built in a "late arrival" buffer into the classes. Since I made ice-breakers mandatory in all of the classes, if someone arrived 10-15 minutes late, they would miss the ice-breaker portion of the class. They would have missed out on the team building or bonding piece, but they would not miss any of the course content. If they arrived after the 15 minute "grace period," they would be directed to contact their manager and would have to reschedule themselves for the class. This typically worked well, and I stopped receiving inquires from my trainers regarding this issue.

QUESTION 7

How do I handle situations when the equipment has technical issues?

Here is where your creative skills and your relationship with your IT Department is critical. (If you don't have a relationship with your IT Department, I suggest you start building one immediately! (I've found snacks and food works best.) When having problems with equipment or any other technical issues, it is important to address most issues right away, depending on the situation. If you are facilitating a Technical Training Class with ten people in a training room with 20 available computers and one computer doesn't work, just have the trainee move to another computer. However, if you have a full class of twenty and ten of the computers are not working, then that is a significant problem. This is why it is so crucial that you come in early to check your equipment and prepare for your classes. Thirty minutes to an hour should suffice, giving you and IT time to fix any issues that may arise. But say you came in early, checked the equipment, everything was fine and just as you get started ten computers (or all twenty computers) stop working. (This has happened to me, and trust me, it will happen to you sometime during your career.) What do you do? You contact IT and then go to Plan B. Here are a few options for Plan B:

1. Move to a different training room or Have the participants "pair up" or "partner up" together until the issue is fixed.
2. Conduct a review session that focuses on how much information people have retained thus far.
3. Facilitate from paper handouts you give the class.
4. Switch Gears! Go outside and conduct Soft Skills Training that does not require computers.
5. Conduct an Activity or Ice-Breaker until the issue is resolved, or until you receive a definitive time for resolution. (You can then decide how to proceed moving forward.)

There are always options in these cases, especially for trainers who look at problems as opportunities to do something differently.

THANK YOU

Thank you for taking the time to read this book. I very much appreciate your doing so. This book is intended to be a platform to build a strong foundation for trainers of all walks of life who are new to the field of training or for those already experienced but would like a refresher. I hope I was able to provide valuable tips and examples of ways to conduct your training sessions and add a little spark to them as well. Training is an art and a science, and there is no "One size fits all" model. There may be times when you wish every class could flow as smoothly as your last one or times when it seems that everything is going wrong. However, when you structure your training program and classes properly, you can minimize the risk of things that can go wrong due to not being prepared or lack of organization. With right amount of structure and preparation, you will create a repeatable model that you, your staff, and organization will appreciate and benefit from. As with anything else, you must continue to learn and evolve to ensure the best possible training outcomes with the latest technology, concepts, and techniques.

If you know of anyone who could benefit from the information in this book, please encourage them to purchase a copy.
Sincerely,

Tavis A. Banks

About the Author

Tavis A. Banks is a Los Angeles native who has spent over 25 years in service to the public. He has focused his energy in Human Resource Development in the healthcare industry specializing in Technical Training, Customer Service Training, and Leadership Development. Early in his career, Tavis found a passion for educating others by developing and empowering new and emerging leaders. Armed with a Master of Arts in Management Degree and a PhD in Common Sense, Tavis has spent the last 15 years dedicated to leading Education and Training Departments in Corporate America. He has helped bridge the gap between front line staff and senior leadership to take their teams to the next level. He has served as a mentor, resource, and collaborator in the training space and maintains an open-door policy with anyone willing to learn, team up, and discuss thoughts on education and training. His passion for teaching has led him to develop training teams at small to large-sized organizations like UnitedHealth Group, OptumRX and AltaMed Health Services. Tavis is also the Chief Creative Officer of Avant Garde Training Group, encouraging people to find new and unusual ways to excel at work and in life through Leadership Development and Training.

QUOTES IN ORDER BY CHAPTER

0. Introduction

"Education must not simply teach work – it must teach Life." W.E.B. DuBois

1. Opening the Class, Introductions and Ice Breakers

"The key to growth is the introduction of high dimensions of consciousness into our awareness." – Lao Tzu

2. Know Your Students Learning Styles

"For the things we have to learn before we can do them, we learn by doing them." – Aristotle

3. Make Learning Fun

"My philosophy is: If you can't have fun, there's no sense in doing it." Paul Walker

4. Soft Skills

"You cannot continuously improve interdependency systems and processes until you progressively perfect interdependent, interpersonal relationships." – Stephen Covey

5. Class Management

Learning is not attained by chance, it must be sought for with ardor and attended with diligence." – Abigail Adams

6. Class Facilitation

"Tell me and I forget, teach me and I may remember, involve me and I learn." – Benjamin Franklin

7. **Designing and Writing Content or Training Material**

   "Of all the life skills available to us, communication is perhaps the most empowering." Bret Morrison

8. **Reviews**

   "In learning you will teach, and in teaching you will learn." – Phil Collins

9. **E-Learning/ Self-Paced Learning**

   "The beautiful thing about learning is that no one can take it away from you." – B.B. King

10. **Closing the Class**

    "The freedom to do your best means nothing unless you are willing to do your best." – General Colin Powell

11. **Epilogue: Did I Answer All of Your Questions?**

    "I hated every minute of training, but I said, don't quit. Suffer now and live the rest of your life as a champion." – Muhammed Ali

REFERENCES

AZ Quotes. (2019, October 1). Retrieved from azquotes.com: https://www.azquotes.com/quote/305594

Beich, E. (2017). *The Art and Science of Training.* Alexandria: ATD Press.

Brainy Quote. (2019, October 13). Retrieved from BrainyQuote.com: https://www.brainyquote.com/quotes/w_e_b_du_bois_745700

Brainy Quote. (2019, October 3). Retrieved from brainyquote.com: https://www.brainyquote.com/quotes/benjamin_franklin_383997

Collins, P. (1999). Son of Man [Recorded by P. Collins]. Germany.

Go Lean Six Sigma. (2019, October 13). Retrieved from goleansixsigma.com: https://goleansixsigma.com/beautiful-thing-learning-nobody-can-take-away-b-b-king/

Good Reads. (2019, September 14). Retrieved from GoodReads.com: https://www.goodreads.com/quotes/4184-for-the-things-we-have-to-learn-before-we-can

Good Reads. (2019, September 23). Retrieved from goodreads.com: https://www.goodreads.com/quotes/26893-the-freedom-to-do-your-best-means-nothing-unless-you

habitsforwellbeing.com. (2019, October 1). Retrieved from Habits for Well Being: https://www.habitsforwellbeing.com/becoming-aware-of-the-monkey-mind/the-key-to-growth-is-the-introduction-of-higher-dimensions-of-consciousness-into-our-awareness-lao-tzu/

John. (2012, September 27). *Challenging Coaching.* Retrieved from challengingcoaching.co.uk: https://challengingcoaching.co.uk/stephen-covey-interdependence-the-deeper-facts/

Lundin, S. C., Paul, H., & Christensen, J. (2000). *FISH! A Proven Way to Boost Morale and Improve Results.* New York: Hyperion.

Madsen, B. T. (2018, July 10). *Book Boon.* Retrieved from bookboon.com: https://bookboon.com/blog/2018/07/10-powerful-quotes-on-soft-skills/

Pass It On . (2019, September 23). Retrieved from passiton.com: https://www.passiton.com/inspirational-quotes/6790-learning-is-not-attained-by-chance-it-must-be

Quotes. (2019, September 27). Retrieved from quotes.net: https://www.quotes.net/quote/49609

Team, T. M. (2015, September 3). *Mind Tools.* Retrieved from MindTools.com: https://www.mindtools.com/pages/article/vak-learning-styles.htm

TrainingIndustry.com. (2019, April 23). Retrieved from Training Industry: https://trainingindustry.com/wiki/outsourcing/size-of-training-industry/

T3

Train the Trainer

10 Things Every Successful Trainer **Must Know**

Tavis A. Banks

Made in United States
Orlando, FL
08 February 2023